"Packed with intelligent, energetic women, Roberts' sisters by blood or by choice, and 'superwomen' in the corridors of social change. . . . Lively reading. . . . [Roberts is] a nurturer, a custodian of time-honored values, an accomplished professional and, in this book, simply, wisely proud to be so."
—*USA Today*

"This book is a celebration of women in all their various roles: mother, sister, civil rights advocate, consumer advocate, first-class mechanic, politician—which Roberts' own mother once was."
—*Chicago Sun-Times*

"Entertaining. . . . Absorbing."
—Associated Press

"Roberts does some serious talkin' 'bout her generation. . . . Combines the personal with the political. . . . Her subject matter intrigues for both her personal spin and the biographies of unusual and powerful women."
—*Los Angeles Times*

"[A] book of inspirational stories of women who have successfully nurtured their children while working outside the home. With humor, honesty and optimism, [Roberts] provides perspective on this balancing act. . . . Encouraging. . . . The most inspirational stories are those of Roberts' own life."
—*Newsday*

"Roberts weaves colorful vignettes with pertinent and interesting facts to show the historic scope of women's accomplishments over many generations. Along the way, Roberts also touches on the important roles women play as sister, mother, daughter, and friend."
—*Rocky Mountain News*

"A tribute . . . which pays homage to those who've come before, and those who're coming along. . . . Highlights the many paths women have pursued over the years."

—*Kansas City Star*

"Heartfelt. . . . Explores the different kinds of work that women do and have done throughout history for their communities and families as well as for themselves and even one another." —*Daily News*

"Roberts knows quite a bit about the various roles that women undertake in a lifetime. . . . This volume of essays and personal insight into various roles of women throughout American history reflects the wisdom of someone who has lived through many changing and challenging roles herself. . . . Roberts concludes that women are the glue that holds a family and society together. Accepting that mantle as it is passed down from generation to generation is a fulfilling and important task."

—*Chattanooga Free Press*

"An artfully arranged collection of vignettes about women's roles, women's lives and women's relationships with one another. . . . Splendidly told. . . . Roberts' message reaches across party, societal and generational lines. . . . It's by providing readers with her own experiences that Roberts grounds the book in the commonality of women's lives. There are moments to which almost all women can relate. . . . A thoughtful, informative, entertaining and evocative book." —*The Hill*

"Vibrant essays. . . . Poignant and personal. . . . Fact-filled portraits . . . delivered in a conversational, often humorous tone."
—*Orange County Register*

"A mix of inspiring personal stories with the stories of women significant in history. It is an attempt to put Roberts' life and the women's movement into a broader context, to assert that women have always played many roles at the same time, to add to the pool of role models."
—*Austin-American Statesman*

"Talk about hats, Cokie Roberts has a closet full."
—*Palm Beach Post*

"Cokie Roberts is a talented political commentator, bringing to her work the common sense of a woman who grew up enjoying a life that fused politics and family. . . . It's no wonder that *We Are Our Mothers' Daughters* is already a bestseller. . . . Amusing anecdotes. . . . Appealing. . . . Inspires."
—*Washington Times*

"Personal anecdotes and inspirational stories of women who have fulfilled their nurturing instincts while working outside the home."
—*People*

About the Author

COKIE ROBERTS is a political commentator for ABC News and a senior news analyst for National Public Radio. From 1996 to 2002, she and Sam Donaldson coanchored the weekly ABC interview program *This Week*.

In addition to broadcasting, Roberts, along with her husband, Steven V. Roberts, writes a weekly column syndicated in newspapers around the country by United Media. Both are also contributing editors to *USA Weekend*, and together they wrote *From This Day Forward*, an account of their now more than forty-year marriage and other marriages in American history. The book immediately went onto the *New York Times* bestseller list. Roberts is also the author of the bestsellers *Founding Mothers* and its companion volume *Ladies of Liberty*. A mother of two and grandmother of six, she lives with her husband in Bethesda, Maryland.

WE ARE OUR

MOTHERS'

DAUGHTERS

Revised and Expanded Edition

Cokie Roberts

HARPER PERENNIAL

NEW YORK • LONDON • TORONTO • SYDNEY • NEW DELHI • AUCKLAND

This book is about women. But it would not be possible without a man. To my husband, Steven—my mentor, my fan, my lover, my muse—this book is dedicated.

HARPER⬤PERENNIAL

A hardcover edition of this book was published in 2009 by William Morrow, an imprint of HarperCollins Publishers.

HarperCollins books may be purchased for educational, business, or sales promotional use. For information please write: Special Markets Department, HarperCollins Publishers, 10 East 53rd Street, New York, NY 10022.

FIRST HARPER PERENNIAL EDITION PUBLISHED 2010.

Library of Congress Cataloging-in-Publication Data is available upon request.

ISBN 978-0-06-171592-1 (pbk.)

10 11 12 13 14 WBC/RRD 10 9 8 7 6 5 4 3 2 1

Contents

Introduction to the Revised Edition

THERE'S A REASON WE CELEBRATE BIRTHDAYS. AS ODD AS IT may sound, that fact has come as a surprise to me. I only realized the truth of it when I was asked to update this book. Of course I know how devoted children are to their birthdays—how they delight in the anticipation of their party, the event itself (with any luck), and, of course, the presents. But they are also excited about the fact that they are turning a year older, working their way up the ladder of humanhood. And they are right. In the first decade, between zero and ten, each year makes a huge difference; kids change almost before our eyes.

And then there are the years between ten and twenty, another time of tremendous change. Though I like teenagers, I'm really glad that my own children will soon be worrying about their teenage children instead of me about them. But from twenty on, it all gets kind of amorphous. And so we hold celebrations to demark the differences whether we are aware of them or not—thirty, forty, fifty, etc. Even as I participated in those rituals for friends and family and occasionally for myself, I didn't have a sense of those markers as milestones—until my mother turned ninety. Then I started telling people, "I think that the years between eighty and ninety are like the years between ten and twenty," in terms of change. Everybody just thinks of old age as old age, I would say, but there's a tremendous difference in that decade. Truer, of course, for some than for others but true nonetheless.

Still, the assignment of taking another look at this book, and expanding it, has forced me to realize that there are great chasms we cross from one decade to the next. Not only does the world change around us—ten years ago we thought a blackberry was a piece of fruit—but we change ourselves. Think of the most common compliment a woman my age receives: "You haven't changed a bit." It's usually not true, but the fact that it's meant to flatter is telling. In fact, I have changed a lot. When I first wrote this book I was in my early fifties and felt like I had finally come into my own. I was old enough and accomplished enough that for the first time in my life, men were taking me seriously. I was anchoring a program on network television and my personal life was on an even, and wonderfully satisfying, keel. My husband of thirty-one years and I were both healthy and happy, my children had each just gotten married, and my mother had just been assigned to a new job as U.S. ambassador to the Vatican. Life was brimming over with possibility.

And I've realized those possibilities. I was able to cut back on my work at ABC in order to do something that I had wanted to do for a long time—get involved in volunteer work. For years I had preached that women of my generation who went from college directly into the workforce had an obligation at some point in our lives to do what many of our mothers did by way of contributing to their communities. Now I can. As everyone who has done it knows, there's nothing more satisfying than helping others. I particularly love my time spent with Save the Children, which does an incredible job around the world and in this country getting children out of poverty and into productive lives. By writing this book, I also unwittingly entered into a whole new career as an author. Since the first edition of *We Are Our Mothers' Daughters* was published I've written three other books, one with my husband about marriage, two about the influential women of early America. The history books launched me into a world of historians that has been a wonderfully welcome addition to my life. And, by far the best of all, I have become a grandmother. My excellent children and children-in-law have brought six fascinating, funny, cuddly creatures into the world. They are pure heaven.

Younger women used to ask me constantly about balancing work and family, and of course I still get those questions frequently, particularly on college campuses and among the young women at work. But slightly older women, women in their forties and especially women in their fifties, now ask me all the time, "What next?" What is the next act after a very busy professional life? I think it's a question well worth contemplating, so that we aren't surprised by the changes in our work lives that will inevitably come. There's still always the question of balance, and it's hard to get it right for more than a year or so at a time, but I am happy with the combination of enterprises that now occupy my life in addition to my role as a reporter—I still feel that sense of possibility.

There are, of course, downsides to the passing years. A cousin who's my contemporary recently joked, "If we wake up at our age and nothing hurts, it means we're dead." In the time since I first wrote this book, I've been treated for breast cancer, I've lost some friends and seen others suffer from devastating illnesses, I've watched my mother and mother-in-law turn into very old ladies. They do remarkably well, but they require a good bit of attention and care— which is only fair after the attention and care they have lavished on us—and there is no denying which way the trajectory is headed. Still, "the mothers" are great inspirations to me, as they pluckily push forward, insisting on enjoying life. They are an always present reminder of the grit and fortitude of the women who came before us. I have come to be a great admirer of those women as I've written more about them, and I think they serve as object lessons for to-day's women—that's why I wrote this book in the first place. The demands on women today can be daunting, but when you compare them to what many of the women before us encountered, they don't seem so bad.

So this little volume tells some stories about the many roles women play, discovered through my own life and the lives of other women, both past and present. Interviews with living women came as part of my work as a reporter. And of course my own stories are just that—my own. But I'm always struck by the similarity in women's stories—whether athletes or scientists, businesswomen or soldiers, politicians or mechanics—no matter how different they may superficially seem. That's because of the thread of continuity with women throughout the ages, the sense that we are doing what women have always done, even as we pioneer our way across cultural divides or declare a revolution.

Caretaking—that's the common thread that runs through these stories. No matter what else women are doing, we are also "mothering"—taking care of somebody or something, and, for the most part, doing it joyously. That's what women have been doing from the beginning and, I believe, will continue to do. I think we've been doing it awfully well for a very long time. And I thought it was time to celebrate that. That's why I wrote this book.

We Are Our Mothers' Daughters

□ □ □

WHAT IS WOMAN'S PLACE? THAT'S BEEN THE HOT QUESTION of my adult life. From the boardrooms to the bedrooms of the country's companies and couples, the debate over the role of women has created enormous upheaval for society and for the family. For women like me, who grew up and graduated from college before the revolution, it's all gotten a little exhausting. We were the vanguard, not necessarily in philosophical terms but in practical ones. Most of us weren't engaged in fighting for the feminist cause, but we were busy—unbelievably busy—living it, either consciously or unconsciously. We went with our shiny degrees pouring into the workforce as the first generation of women with the law on our side. When I graduated from Wellesley in

1964 it was perfectly legal to discriminate against women in the workplace. Help Wanted ads in the newspapers were divided into "Male," "Female," "White," "Colored." When we applied for jobs, the men we were applying to regularly and with no embarrassment told us, "We don't hire women to do that." But the 1964 Civil Rights Act was passed that summer and, though it took a while for any of us to realize it, the workplace terrain underwent a seismic shift. (The men who wrote the Civil Rights Act had no intention of changing the lives of women, and therefore men, so dramatically, but that's a tale for another place in these pages.)

We were the pioneers—or so we thought. And in many ways we were. We were the first women at almost everything we did, and most of us often had the experience of being the only woman in the room. Unlike the few women who preceded us in the world of work, who in most cases were singular obstacle-leaping females, we arrived as an entire generation of educated and, in our minds at least, equal-to-men women. We have the scars to show that we knocked down barriers rather than jumped over them, making it easier for the women who followed us. (We've been known to grow a little grumpy over the ingratitude of young women, for their sometimes smug assumption that all that "woman stuff" is passé, ancient history. We find ourselves muttering, like the Wicked Witch of the West, "Just you wait, my pretty.") The brave new world we were forging took its toll—many of our youthful, preliberation marriages didn't survive. The rules changed so fundamentally from the ones in place on our wedding days that it took more than the usual amount of adaptation to make those unions work. I'm one of the lucky ones. At the age of eighteen I spotted the perfect husband, and finally convinced him to propose when I was an almost-over-the-hill twenty-two. With good senses of humor, and incredible generosity on his part, Steven and I have happily managed for more than forty years to make it over the shoals of constantly shifting expectations.

Now here's our generation, women in our sixties, with grown daughters faced with the challenges of work and family. There's a lot of reassessment going on, and a lot of rewriting of history. There's also a lot of foolish rehashing of old debates, as privileged women who have the choice of whether to earn a paycheck engage in finger-pointing at women who make different choices than they do. I must admit this often vituperative argument—the so-called mommy wars—about staying home versus going to work makes me nuts. It's not men who are doing this to women; it's women who are doing it to one another, trying to validate the decisions they make by denigrating the decisions of others.

Over the decades, as I witnessed and participated in this great social movement of the twentieth century, I had only one real fear for women: that we would lose our sense of perspective. Our great strength, in my view, has been our ability to see beyond the concerns of the day. As the nurturers, the caregivers, we have always worried about the future—what it will mean for the children—and as the custodians and carriers of the culture, we've carefully kept alive the past. I was afraid that we might become so involved in the daily demands of the world of work that we would break that thread of connection to generations of women before us. I greatly admire the way men seize the moment, take on the tasks of the day with single-minded purpose. But that is not for us; women have traditionally been multiple-minded. And so we still are, thank God. We, of course, do what the job—whatever it is—requires, but often with some other concern nagging at the backs of our brains.

Instead of this being some early twenty-first-century definition of life on the distaff side, I would argue that it's always been this way—that women have always played many roles at the same time. For years my mother kept telling me that it's nothing new to have women as soldiers, as diplomats, as politicians, as revolutionaries, as explorers, as founders of large institutions, as leaders in business; that the women of my generation did not invent the wheel. In the past women might not have had the titles, she painstakingly and patiently explained, but they did the jobs that fit those descriptions. Now I'm finally old enough, and have had enough life experience of my own, to listen to my mother. In her nineties, she maddeningly responds to almost all "new" developments with some similar story from the past, concluding with her favorite expression, *"Plus ça change, plus c'est la même chose."* As I've learned the stories of the women in this book, the women from our past and today's women following in their footsteps, I've come more and more to appreciate my mother's wisdom.

When we lived in Greece in the 1970s we used to go to the beach at Marathon. (We had to dodge the runners on the highway retracing the original race to Athens, blissfully unaware, it seems, that the man they were imitating dropped dead on arrival.) At first I marveled at the fact that we regularly went swimming at this place that I had read about in history books ever since I was a little girl. Looking out to sea, I could imagine the frightening Persian fleet attacking, the brave Athenian soldiers defending their democracy. A great mound that was supposed to cover the Persian dead stood as a reminder of the oft-told tales of the courageous deeds of those long-ago men. After we had been going to Marathon for a while, we found nestled in the hills another site, one that never made the history books but made me marvel more. It dated back thousands of years earlier than the famous battle, and a tiny museum had been erected to display the findings. Here was nothing of heroic dimensions, nothing on a grand scale: in one case, needles, buttons; in another, jewelry, pots for makeup; in another, frying pans and toys. Here the objects from the everyday lives of women from thousands of years ago overwhelmed me with their familiarity. I could have opened the cases, put on their jewels, taken up their tools, and picked up where they left off without a moment's hesitation or confusion. What was left from the lives of the men? Objects of war and objects of worship, recognizable for soldiers and priests, but what of the others? That little museum has always symbolized for me the great strength of women. We are connected throughout time and regardless of place. We are our mothers' daughters.

Sister

❏   ❏   ❏

WHEN MY OLDER SISTER DIED SHE WAS YOUNGER THAN I AM
now. Any woman who's been even slightly close to her big
sister knows what that means—it means uncharted territory. It never occurred to me that this would happen, that
I'd be on my own in a way that I never expected. Until Barbara died, it had never occurred to me that I had not been
on my own. I had not realized, did not have a clue, how
much I counted on her to do it first.

All of my life she had been there, lording it over me and
loving me, pushing me around and protecting me. Those
elusive early childhood memories that shimmer to the sur-
face when summoned all involve her. Running to her when
the dog next door jumped up and grabbed my two-year-old

hair in its teeth. Barbara running to our mother complaining that if I insisted on putting on doll clothes, couldn't I be confined to the backyard. Going to school where she, four years older, shepherded me from room to room. Getting her out of classes to pull my baby teeth. Huddling together against the brother between us in age, the common enemy.

She excelled at everything, always. She was the president of the class, of the school; the top student; the best writer, debater. She was also very beautiful. Every so often a thoughtless teacher would ask, Why can't you be more like your sister? But I don't ever remember being jealous of her. I just desperately wanted to please her, and I often didn't. She had the ability to push all my buttons, the way most women (including my daughter) complain their mothers do. Because she was there between us, my mother and I never experienced the usual mother-daughter tensions. That gift lives on after her. We had such a good time together that she once said, "If we lived next door to each other, we'd never go to work." It's true that I never laugh as hard as I do with the women in my family—my sister, mother, daughter. Fortunately for her community, I never lived next door and Barbara toiled tirelessly as a public servant taking painstaking care of everyone else until the day she died.

The dying part was so profound, and so profoundly weird, that it taught me a great deal about sisterhood, in all its meanings. One fine day in October 1989 Barbara and I in our separate cities, unbeknownst to each other, went like responsible middle-aged ladies for our annual mammo-grams. In retrospect, it reminded me of the years when we lived in rooms next door to each other and would occasion-ally emerge at the same time humming the same bar of the same tune under our breaths. But this time nothing else was the same. The technician told me the usual "Check with us in a few days." The person who read the pictures of Barba-ra's breast clucked and sent her in for more X rays—her lungs, her liver, her bones, her brain. (She called these, plus the endless CT scans and MRIs that would come over the course of the next year, and that we carried from doctor to doctor, "The Inside Story of Barbara Sigmund.")

She phoned me the next morning. "I have cancer every-where," she said. "You have to help me tell Mamma." I got off the phone and crumpled into Steven's arms. "We're go-ing to lose her. Nobody has cancer that many places and lives," I sobbed. Her friend and neighbor, a radiologist, told her that without treatment she had perhaps six months to live. With treatment, who knew? Maybe miracles! She had turned fifty only a few months before. We arranged for me to go to my mother's office at a free time in her schedule, and Barbara agreed to keep her phone free at that time. (Free times and free phones are rare in our family.) The plan was for me to be with Mamma while my sister told her the dread diagnosis. This was Barbara's attempt to correct what she thought was a bad mistake seven years earlier when she had reached Mamma alone at the end of a workday and blurted out that she had to have her eye removed. That, of course, should have served as a warning to us. But the doctor at the time told us that the chances of the melanoma behind her left eye recurring were less than if she had never had cancer at all. And Barbara handled the whole thing with such incredible style and panache, sporting spectacular sequined or feathered eye patches with evening dresses, matching an outfit with a color-coordinated patch for everyday wear. She never seemed sick, just understandably tired in the middle of her political campaigns, and the famous five-year mark for cancer patients had passed successfully.

The appointed hour with my mother came at about eleven thirty in the morning. "Perfect," pronounced my Jewish husband, "you tell her and then the two of you go straight to noon Mass." And that's what happened. Then began the pathetic odyssey of people living under the death sentence of widespread cancer. First, trying to get information: What were the treatments? Where were they? What was the success rate? What we learned eventually, certainly not right away: When it comes to this highly experimental stuff, everybody's guessing.

After the initial terror, we settled into something of a routine. Barbara and her husband, Paul, would travel from their home in Princeton, New Jersey, to a hospital in Philadelphia. I would meet them there and spend the nights in her room, watching poison chemicals drip into my sister's body. Mamma would come up from Washington for most of the time as well. Then we would head back to Princeton, and Mamma or I or my brother's wife, our other sister, would stay with Barbara until she was feeling better.

In those months, circles upon circles of sisters emerged. In the hospital, one of the doctors on Barbara's team was a woman whose willingness to tell us the truth was something I will forever value. It's not that the male doctors weren't caring; it's just that they couldn't deal with what they saw as their own failure, their inability to lick the disease. Another woman doctor, a pathologist who had nothing to do with the case, adopted Mamma and me when she saw us in the cafeteria. She would come visit in the room and cheer us up—yes, a cheery pathologist!—during her time "off." Then there were the legions of nurses, those sensible, funny, wonderful women who have the strength to deal with death on a daily basis.

Back in Princeton, the women of the town swung into action. Each gave according to her ability, to us who were so needy. People organized to cook and bring food, to visit, to run errands, to help with the mail that pours in when a public figure's illness is announced. And this for a full year! Most of the time Barbara kept working at her job as mayor, but the women in her office often had to take up the slack during the times she was in the hospital. With the attendant immune problems from chemotherapy, hospital stays became common for both of us as I took on the role of what Barbara called her "private duty sister." Again, there were a few fabulous men who gave of themselves completely, including their blood and, more important, their time. But my brother-in-law, the most giving and suffering of us all, noticed how it was women who kept Barbara and him going.

While these women tended to Barbara, others tended to Mamma and me. Our colleagues, busy professional women all, were incredibly attentive. The support systems and sisterhood of women working together had never been more important. My two closest friends arranged their vacation schedules to make sure that I would never be alone if I needed them, and they filled in the blanks that I was leaving at work without my even knowing about it. My mother's colleagues were members of Congress—talk about busy women! But they were there for her throughout that long year, and after Barbara died they came back from their campaigns—several of them were running for the Senate—to hold a private Mass in the Congresswomen's Reading Room at the Capitol (a room now named for my mother, the only room in the Capitol named for a woman).

Over the summer, as her condition deteriorated, the treatments stopped, but better therapy arrived when Barbara's three boys came home. All in their early twenties then, they found ways to be in Princeton to the utter delight of their dying mother. When the fall came, and she waved them off, she knew she was seeing them for the last time.

Then it became time for the women to gather around.

And they did. The hairdresser would come to the house and regale us with stories as she tried to keep Barbara's head beautiful above her sad, sick body. My daughter, Rebecca, in her junior year at Princeton University, became her aunt's nurse of choice in those final few weeks. The Religious of the Sacred Heart, the nuns who had taught us as children and were now our friends and contemporaries and confidantes, would come by with Holy Communion and hilarious conversation. A dear friend devoted herself full-time to Barbara, defining sisterhood by action, not the accident of blood. The oncologist, a woman, visited and explained to us what to expect when Barbara died, an act of simple kindness that somehow helped. Barbara made it possible for us all to learn through her suffering, giving us mainly unspoken lessons in how to die with dignity. Some of her instructions were clearly spoken. She planned her funeral, making sure it would be right, not leaving it to chance, by which, I only half joked, she meant her family. "Let me introduce myself," I would jest, "I am Chance." She also wrote bald, unsentimental poems in what she called "A Diary of a Fatal Illness" and lived to see them published and read at the local Arts Council. Some medical schools now use her poetry to teach students about dying.

My mother had announced that she would resign from Congress at the end of her term. She didn't say it at the time, but she did it so she could be with Barbara. The cancer, with no respect for schedule, deprived Mamma of that opportunity. I had expected to take a leave of absence to care for my sister at the end—just give me a signal, I said to the doctors. They did, the day before she died. The next day, Barbara and I had a good laugh as I was combing her hair, which hadn't been colored in a while. "I think we're seeing your natural hair color for the first time since you were fifteen," I teased. But despite attempts at humor, my mother could hear a change in my voice on the telephone. She arrived that night and had a little visit before bedtime. Barbara died before morning.

THE FIRST TIME I PICKED UP THE PHONE TO CALL HER CAME in response to a story on page one of that day's *New York Times*. The subject: childbirth for postmenopausal women. The article dutifully reported the how, where, who, and when. But it left out what was for me, and I knew would be for her, the key question—why? She had a whole routine about how women she knew were producing their own grandchildren with these late-in-life babies. Ready to have a good giggle, I dialed her number before I remembered she wouldn't be there to share my astonishment. The shock of her absence made me feel very alone.

At some point during Barbara's illness I began preparing myself for a different vision of my old age. Without really thinking about it, I had always assumed we'd occupy adjacent rockers on some front porch, either literally or figuratively. Now one of those chairs would be empty. Intellectually

I understood that. But every time some new thing happens that she's not here for, emotionally it hits me all over again—that sense of charting new territories without the map of my older sister.

And here's what I didn't expect at all—not only was I robbed of some part of my future, I was also deprived of my past. When a childhood memory needed checking, all my life I had simply run it by Barbara. Now there's no one to set me straight. My mother and brother can help some. My brother and I have, in fact, grown a good deal closer since our sister died; after all, without him, I would not only not have a sister, I would not be a sister. But Tommy didn't go to school with me, share a room with me, grow up female with me. Though I love him dearly, he is not my sister.

There it is. For all of the wonderful expressions of sisterhood from so many sources, for all of the support I both receive and provide, for all of the friendships I cherish, it's not the same. I only had one sister.

This is the only chapter of this book I have not revised. What more is there to say? As I write this, it has been eighteen years since Barbara died and I still miss her terribly. It's not the same acute pain, of course, as that of a new loss. But every so often something will happen to bring the full force of grief rushing right back in. One day recently in the chapel at Stone Ridge, the school we both loved, two little girls stood out from the choir to sing a duet in harmony. Unbidden, a memory of a similar duet with a terrified ten-year-old me carrying the alto part all by myself shot to the front of my brain. My big sister had made sure to position herself in one of the first few rows of the audience so that I could see her smile of encouragement, getting me through the performance. Sitting in the chapel those many decades later, I couldn't stop the tears.

My granddaughters are the same difference in age that Barbara and I were. When I was staying with them not too long ago, I was totally unprepared when something the older one said about her little sister slammed me in the back of the head with love and longing for my sister. And of course Barbara's own granddaughters—her boys produced the girls she always wanted—her own granddaughters break my heart.

POLITICIAN

■　　　■　　　■

WHY HASN'T AMERICA ELECTED A WOMAN PRESIDENT? I'M asked that question all the time, with the questioner often pointing to the fact that far less "advanced" countries— India, Pakistan, Argentina—have seen women at their helms. It's a question that became more insistent during the 2008 campaign when Hillary Clinton came close to winning the Democratic presidential nomination and Sarah Palin clinched the number two spot on the Republican ticket. Of course, neither the New York senator nor the Alaska governor won; and their defeats might make victory more problematic for future female candidates. As Ruth Mandel, a founder of Rutgers University's Center for American Women and Politics, told the *Chicago Tribune,* Clinton's arduous campaign "hardly made it look like something that most mortals . . . male or female would want to take on," adding, "I see her as Wonder Woman blazing the trail, but I don't know what that means for mortals coming up behind her."

Not only might aspiring female politicians be discouraged by the defeat of the two high-profile women of 2008, their losses might also convince male politicians that women are risky candidates not worth supporting. I find those possibilities more than a little depressing. In all the appropriate euphoria on election night 2008 about the history-making nature of the election of the first African American president, and all the commentary that now every child in America knows he can grow up to be anything he wants to be, I kept thinking, "Unless he is a she." So I want to see a woman elected president before I die—not only because I think it's important for our girls to see someone like them achieve the highest position possible, but also because I know that electing women makes a difference to America's families. Because I have reported on Congress and politics for decades now, I can point to evidence of the effect of women in office. But it doesn't take someone who sees politicians up close and personally to know that electing women matters—I think women voters also understand that their sisters in the legislative chambers look out for them. How else can you explain the fact that women often loudly proclaim that they hate politics and politicians, but are thrilled when a woman is elected? Logically, you'd think they would want women to stay away from something they see as tainted and tawdry. But no, our guts tell us that it's better for us and better for politics if women participate. And if what you're interested in is government action on behalf of women and children, there's plenty of data to tell us our guts are right.

First, let me disassociate myself, as the politicians would say, from the sentiments I've just described. I don't hate politics and politicians; in my case, it would mean hating my family and everything it stands for, and I most decidedly do not. My father, Hale Boggs, went to Congress before I was born; my mother was elected to fill his seat after he disappeared in an airplane over Alaska. My childhood home was filled with politicians my entire life—they were friends, courtesy "uncles," fascinating storytellers, dedicated public servants, and a few genuine wackos. As children, my brother and sister and I thought of people like Sam Rayburn, Lyndon Johnson, Hubert Humphrey, and Gerald Ford as family friends who would come by for a casual dinner picked from the vegetable garden. We knew a lot of women who were politically active, our mother chief among them, but we didn't know many women in office. My sister-in-law, Barbara, Tommy's wife, whom I've known my entire life and for whom the suffix "in-law" seems ridiculous, worked as a new bride for Julia Butler Hansen, congresswoman from Washington. But by and large in my experience women were behind the scenes in politics, doing most of the work and getting none of the glory. My mother organized voter registration drives, traveled the country making speeches, advancing candidates, producing rallies in every presidential election of her adult life. She ran my father's campaigns, aided in his offices, presided over political institutions in Washington. In the years she did her stint as congressional wife, there was no political push from either party to get women involved either as candidates or as voters. Politicians had decided there was no such thing as the "women's vote."

Bear with me here for a little history. After the long push for women's suffrage finally succeeded in 1920 (don't you love the way history books say, "And then women got the right to vote," like it happened overnight?), the men in Congress got scared. They figured this new group of voters would demand all kinds of legislation to help women and children, so they introduced more than one hundred bills to do just that. The debate over the first federal measure dealing with health care, the Sheppard-Towner Act, made the cause and effect stunningly clear. We better do this, said supporters of the legislation designed to provide maternal and child health education, or the newly enfranchised women will punish us. As one congressman bluntly explained: "If Members could have voted in the cloakroom it would have been killed." Instead, the health care measure was signed into law on November 23, 1921, and no one was punished. But no one was rewarded either. The politicians saw no payback at the polls. Women had pushed for the vote in order to bring about social reforms, but when politicians took the first tentative steps toward enacting the kind of change women wanted, they were greeted with silence from the ladies' gallery. The promise, or threat, of the women's vote had failed to materialize.

Many women didn't vote at all, after working so hard for the right, and those who did voted no differently from men. So the politicians soon lost interest. When the Sheppard-Towner Act came up for renewal in 1928, it was defeated. And in the 1930s, Depression-era laws were downright hostile to women. The Economy Act of 1932 made it illegal for the spouse of a federal employee to hold a government job and mandated that wives of employed men would go first in cutbacks of federal jobs. Fifteen hundred people lost their jobs virtually overnight—75 percent of them were women—and more women resigned to protect their husbands' positions. The National Industrial Recovery Act of 1933 wrote into law that many women in government jobs would make less than men doing the same work. It took almost thirty years to right that wrong.

So began a pattern repeated several times in the short political history of American women—expectations raised, then dashed, as women failed to deliver at the ballot box. In the early days of public-opinion polling, the most common answer from women to questions about their views on public policy issues was: "Wait until my husband gets home." Still, women's organizations—the League of Women Voters,

Business and Professional Women, the American Association of University Women, the YWCA—women in labor unions, and women in political parties kept up the pressure on politicians throughout the 1930s, 1940s, and 1950s, working for better health and safety, against child labor, and for equal pay.

Suddenly, in the 1960s, their efforts started paying off. The Equal Pay Act passed in 1963 (it had first been introduced in 1945!), followed the next year by the single most important law affecting women as workers—the 1964 Civil Rights Act. That's actually a funny story. The old curmudgeonly warhorse Howard Smith of Virginia tried desperately to kill the landmark law. He knew the bill banning racial discrimination was barreling down the track following Martin Luther King's march on Washington, President Kennedy's assassination, and President Johnson's full-throated endorsement. So Smith cooked up a little mischief. His colleagues might be crazy enough, in his view, to end legal discrimination on the basis of race, but they certainly wouldn't go for anything that outlawed discrimination against women. Hoping to divide his opponents and bring down the bill, Smith decided that *he* would make the speech introducing an amendment to the section on employment being pushed by some congresswomen—the addition of the word *sex* to the language forbidding discrimination on the basis of race, color, creed, or national origin. Raucous laughter greeted his speech, causing Michigan Democrat Martha

Griffiths to chastise her colleagues: "I suppose that if there had been any necessity to have pointed out that women were a second-class sex, the laughter would have proved it." She warned every man in the chamber that a vote against the amendment was "a vote against his wife, or his widow, or his daughter, or his sister."

Howard Smith guessed wrong with his little joke; there was no derailing civil rights that year, and Democratic and Republican women in Congress maneuvered to keep the word *sex* in the bill up to the very end. (In recent years, the Lyndon Johnson telephone tapes have been released by his presidential library. When I was doing an NPR piece on the fortieth anniversary of the Civil Rights Act, I heard the call from Texas Democrat Jack Brooks to the president telling him that the House had passed the bill. When Johnson asked if there was anything in it that might cause problems in the Senate, Brooks said something like, "Oh, there's something about women, but I don't think we have to worry about that." So much for the legislation that changed the face of employment for women in America.) Howard Smith's plot that backfired made it illegal for employers to say ever again, "We don't hire women to do that."

When I graduated from college in June 1964, I heard that miserable sentence all the time, and it made me crazy, but there was nothing I could do about it. By the end of the summer, I would have grounds for a lawsuit. Of course, most employers didn't know that, and young women like me would never have acted on our newfound right. But many other women did, thank heavens. Throughout the 1960s, brave women sued and won against hundreds of companies that practiced sex discrimination. And a new women's political movement got going as well, putting the heat on Congress again to pay attention to women's issues. In 1972 more legislation passed than in the previous ten years combined—including the first federal child care act and the bill banning discrimination in education, including sports. That measure, called Title IX, had the effect of creating whole generations of women athletes. Then came equal credit, which had the effect of creating whole generations of female business owners. Why did all this legislation finally pass? What happened to turn Congress around after its disillusionment with women as a political force? Women's lives had changed, that's what happened. Women were graduating from college, having fewer babies, and getting divorced in numbers never known before. And what did that mean? It meant women in the workplace. And what did they find there? Glaring—and legal—inequality. For a long time, women just accepted their second-class status as inevitable, that's the way things were, there was nothing to be done about it. But then women started talking to each other, and then they started organizing. And when they came to Congress with their complaints, they found a few female souls ready to listen, and act.

When the first woman, Republican Jeannette Rankin,

was elected to Congress in 1916, she carried with her from the wilds of Montana a full bag of female concerns. She also carried celebrity status—she got offers to write a column (which she did, for Chicago's *Sunday Herald*), to make speeches (which she did, for five hundred dollars an appearance!), and to get married (which she did not). Letters and visitors poured into her office, making it necessary for her to crowd three secretaries into her one room. Rankin understood that the glare of the limelight meant her every move would be watched: "It was very hard for me to understand, to realize that it made a difference what I did and didn't do from then on." What she did, of course, as the sole congresswoman elected from one of the few states that allowed women to vote, was push for national suffrage. She also worked for women's health education (what became the Sheppard-Towner Act), against child labor, and for the establishment of child care centers for working mothers—this in 1918! As World War I heated up, she militated for equal job opportunities and pay for women in war-related industries. But she also militated against war, and her highly unpopular vote on the declaration of war against Germany—"I want to stand by my country, but I cannot vote for war"—cost her her seat. Rankin was defeated at the end of one term and embarked on a career lobbying against war and for social welfare. With Europe once again at war, she ran again for Congress and won in 1940 (the same year my father went to Washington, so my mother knew her!). After Pearl Harbor she stood as the sole vote against the declaration of World War II, making her own declaration: "As a woman I can't go to war, and I refuse to send anyone else." Again she served only one term, but her statue stands in the new Capitol Visitor Center, greeting all who come to learn about Congress.

Over the next few decades after Rankin's groundbreaking election, women dribbled into Congress, many of them the widows of congressmen. Most arrived with no agenda for women in mind, but they all found, once they started serving, that women all over the country came to them with their concerns. When you call the roll of women in Congress in the twenties, thirties, forties, and fifties, you find that they toiled in the corridors and the cloakrooms of the Capitol pressing their colleagues on equal pay, tax relief for single parents and working mothers, school lunches, consumer safety, food stamps, and the place of women in the military. Equally important, they came to the table of government with different sensibilities. Women simply experience life differently from men. And these mothers, sisters, daughters, and wives brought and continue to bring the perspectives of those roles to governing. The men they serve with aren't always ready to recognize the value of those perspectives. In her book *Know Your Power,* Nancy Pelosi tells a story about a group of members who regularly had dinner together, including a few congresswomen. The men, said Pelosi, never asked the women's opinions, but the women would occasionally "chime in if we wanted to."

Then one night when the subject turned to childbirth and the men all started trading gory stories, the women were convinced that this was a place where the men might actually solicit their views: "It never happened. Eleven childbirths among us, and not once did it occur to the men that we might have something to contribute on the subject, or that perhaps we wanted to *change* the subject. They didn't have a clue." When the women later called the men on their cluelessness, they denied all. But, Pelosi concludes, "I didn't come to Congress to change the attitudes of men. I came to change the policies of our country."

And that's what congresswomen have been doing for decades. When my mother was elected to Congress in 1973, she had just learned firsthand that many widows lost their credit along with their mates. It was bad enough to lose my father, then the majority leader of the House of Representatives, who disappeared in an airplane over Alaska and was never found. To add insult to sorrow, Mamma found herself dealing with banks and creditors, trying to explain her peculiar situation. When the time came to declare Daddy's congressional seat vacant, no one questioned that Mamma was the best person for the office. She simply remembers that when the governor called the election, she responded like an old warhorse without ever thinking about it. My sister, a politician herself, told our mother that the hardest part of her job would be voting. She was so used to smoothing things over for my father, acting as a go-between among the factions, that she would have a hard time declaring herself, coming down on one side versus the other. As Barbara told her, "Mamma, there's no 'maybe' button."

That *was* hard for her. But service on the Banking and Currency Committee was not. It became a perfect place to fix the credit discrimination she and friends of hers whose husbands had died or deserted them had experienced. As my mother tells the story, the committee was considering legislation barring banks from denying anyone a loan because of race, national origin, or creed. According to Mamma, she sneaked into a back room, wrote the words "or sex or marital status" in longhand into the text of the bill, made copies, and then brought them back to her colleagues, saying in her sweet, southern way, "I'm sure the omission of women was just an oversight on your part." It helps to have a woman in the right place at the right time. A few years later, Steve and I bought my mother's house (or evicted her, as she jokingly put it; at least I think she was joking), and she moved downtown to a condominium. It seemed to be taking an inordinately long time to get her loan approved, so she called the bank and said, "I find it passing strange that I haven't gotten my mortgage, and since my assets and income are a matter of public record, I have to assume that it's because I'm female and elderly. As an author of the equal credit bill, that concerns me." Needless to say, she got her loan that afternoon. Several years after that, when I was refinancing the house, the lawyer was shoving pieces of paper in front of me to sign.

"What's this one?" I asked. "Oh, that's nothing," he replied. "It just says that we didn't discriminate against you on the basis of sex, age, or race." "That's not nothing," I sternly retorted. "That's my mother's legislation."

If it helps to have a woman in the right place at the right time, it helps even more if that woman is backed by millions of women voters who might retaliate politically—throw the bums out, or in. That's what the politicians worried about back in the 1920s. Finally, in 1980, sixty years after suffrage, they had reason to worry. In that election, for the first time, women turned out to vote in the same proportion as men and they voted differently from men. Thus was born the now famous gender gap, which has become such a fixture in American politics. There's a lot of confusion about the term *gender gap*. It does not mean that women vote for women. It's simply a description of the difference between the way men and women vote. In that election a majority of the men and a majority of the women voted for Ronald Reagan, but women did so by a smaller percentage than men did: 55 percent of men backed the Republican candidate versus 47 percent of women. The space between those percentages was christened the *gender gap*.

The fact that women had voted differently stirred up a good deal of interest among politicians—but nowhere near as much interest as they showed two years later. Then women, who turned out to vote in greater numbers than men, managed to elect politicians who lost the male vote. If the election that year had been reserved for men only, Mario Cuomo would not have been governor of New York, Jim Blanchard would not have been governor of Michigan, and twenty-six Republicans who lost their seats in the House of Representatives would probably have kept them. Women stirred by the recession, as the last hired, first fired, and upset about threats to Social Security, since they make up the bulk of recipients, voted against Republicans. And boy did the politicians take notice! It was as if a spotlight suddenly shone on everyone in a skirt in Congress. Men rushed to join the Congressional Caucus for Women's Issues. They followed the lead of the congresswomen in passing a passel of bills helping women and children: public service jobs, pension reform, child support enforcement, and a crackdown on domestic violence. Some of those bills had been hanging around for decades, but the congresswomen carried the finally realized power of the women's vote onto the floors of the House and Senate and crisscrossed the chambers, working both sides of the aisles to get the legislation passed. Republican women were invited for regular sessions at the White House, where they were asked to give tutorials on "what women want." (One day close to Christmas, then congresswoman, now senator, Olympia Snowe told me she was going to the White House that night for one of those sessions. When I asked her the next day how it went, she replied, "I realized I couldn't go because I hadn't bought any Christmas presents. I spent the evening at

Toys R Us." That's what I mean about men and women experiencing the world differently.) What a heady time it was for women politicians! So much so that Democrats decided to put a woman, New York congresswoman Geraldine Ferraro, on the presidential ticket—hoping she would give them some small shot at ousting Ronald Reagan. Women around the country cheered for the first female in the second spot, but they didn't vote for her. The majority still went for Reagan and Bush over Mondale and Ferraro. And the day after the 1984 election, when the Democrats had lost forty-nine states, the political pros once again started focusing all their attention on the white male vote. So it happened again. Expectations raised, expectations dashed. But this time, even though politicians lost interest in women, there was no going back to the old days. Two things had changed since the 1930s: one, the women's vote had elected four U.S. senators who lost the male vote in 1984; and two, there were enough women in Congress determined to keep pressing for their agenda.

Let's take a moment here to explain what the women's vote is and what it is not. It is not a vote based on abortion or other so-called women's issues. All of our polling tells us that men and women vote exactly the same on those questions. The women's vote is an economic vote. Women not only make less money than men, they are also much more likely to be the beneficiaries of government programs or the caretakers of beneficiaries. That's particularly true of Social

Security and Medicare (we wish men lived as long as we do, but they don't), but it's also true of food stamps and welfare. Women often work for government-funded institutions—schools, nursing homes, hospitals, day care centers, museums, social services offices, arts councils—so they tend to be less wary of government than many men are. That makes women more likely to vote for the Democratic Party's candidate. Both parties hate the fact that, all things being equal, the women's vote goes Democratic: Republicans for the very sensible reason that it means the majority of voters go for the opposition party; Democrats because they worry that it means real men don't like Democrats. And there's a lot of truth to that. But both parties also know that they need the women's vote to win elections.

Because of that, women in Congress managed through the 1980s to drip their issues over their colleagues' heads like a form of water torture. Drip, child care, drip, child support enforcement, drip, mammography coverage by Medicare, drip, increased funding for breast cancer research, drip, commercial credit for women. It's not that the men don't care about those issues, it's just that they don't put them at the top of their priority lists the way women do. And the congresswomen organized across party lines, consciously placing their members on as many committees as possible in order to keep up the pressure for their programs. But it was tough because there were so few of them, never more than twenty-nine in the House, two in the Senate.

Every election, we women in the press would write hopefully that this was the Year of the Woman. The results embarrassed us over and over again. Finally, in 1992, it came true. More women won in that one election than had been elected in any *decade* before that. Before 1992 a *total* of only sixteen women had served in the Senate. But when Congress convened in 1993, it was with forty-seven women in the House, eight in the Senate. What a moment! It seemed like women were everywhere all of a sudden, and they were all kinds of women—white, black, Hispanic, Asian American—even though the percentages were still tiny. For the first time it was possible to measure statistically what we knew instinctively—that women in office make a difference on key issues. That's been tracked in the state legislatures for years, but there were never enough women at the national level to be able to say it with certainty. One good example: gun control. Women see this as a "mommy issue"—no machine guns on playgrounds, good idea! The ban on assault weapons would never have passed Congress had there been fewer women in 1993. Only 23 percent of Republican men voted for it, but 67 percent of Republican women did. On the Democratic side, 89 percent of the women voted to get rid of the high-powered weapons, compared with 72 percent of the men. It was a close vote where women made the difference. Another landmark piece of legislation passed that year, the Family and Medical Leave Act, was pushed and prodded onto the congressional calendar by two women in the House—Republican Marge Roukema of New Jersey and Democrat Patricia Schroeder of Colorado. The law gives workers the assurance that their jobs will be waiting for them if they take up to twelve weeks of unpaid time off to care for a family member, including a newborn or adopted baby, or for themselves. By the time the bill-signing ceremony at the White House took place, the measure was so popular that the men in Congress took all the credit for it, causing Schroeder to gently grouse: "Often you see women start the issue, educate on the issue, fight for the issue, and then when it becomes fashionable, men push us aside."

The American political scene is so volatile, and we in the media are so ready to look for something new to characterize each election, that the 1992 Year of the Woman quickly gave way to the 1994 focus on "the angry white male" and then the 1996 "soccer mom" followed by the 2000 "NASCAR dad" and then the 2004 "security mom." Each was an attempt to describe key voters in those elections and they reflect the ups and downs of women's influence on the political scene. But in each election women held their own in Congress, and the increased numbers of Republican women meant their voices were heard in party councils. Because of the concerted effort of those congresswomen, Republicans included a strong child support enforcement section in the welfare reform bill.

Anyone who doubts the power of the women's vote just needs to look at the 1996 election. Women took center stage at the party conventions, giving me a giggle at the thought of the ghosts of the old pols of the past hovering in the rafters of those convention halls, celestial cigars clenched in their teeth, puzzling over speeches about the problems of coping with work and children. First Lady Hillary Clinton even threw in the difficulty of getting the dog to the vet. Republican Bob Dole was trailing so badly among women in the polls that his fellow party members in Congress labored to shore up their own female support and passed a bundle of bills to do just that. Since two-thirds of the people who earn a minimum wage are women, Republicans voted to increase the minimum wage. They also expanded health care coverage, mandated to insurance companies that they cover at least a forty-eight-hour hospital stay for new mothers (to put an end to what President Clinton so elegantly called "drive-by deliveries"), and they added domestic violence to the list of crimes that would make a person ineligible for gun ownership. And it worked. Republicans held on to Congress, while women voted overwhelmingly Democratic for president, giving Bill Clinton a sixteen-point edge over his opponent. Had women's suffrage never been enacted, Bob Dole would have been elected, since he managed to edge out the sitting president by one point among men. After both of those contenders left government, we saw something we've never seen before in American politics, as each of their wives went to the Senate—Democrat Hillary Rodham Clinton from New

York and Republican Elizabeth Hanford Dole, a former cabinet officer in two Republican administrations, from North Carolina. Dole was subsequently defeated, by another woman, in 2008, and Clinton went on to run for president and then accepted the job of secretary of state. But for a few years the two women wore the mantle of the politician in the family while their husbands sat on the sidelines.

The gender gap narrowed somewhat in the 2000 election, with Vice President Al Gore carrying women by eleven points over Republican George W. Bush. But as president, Bush worked to woo women, as he had successfully done when governor of Texas—particularly more economically secure married women. And he won those married women in 2004 while losing the overall women's vote by only 3 percent. In 2008, with hard economic times and an unpopular war in Iraq, women again flocked to the Democratic candidate, Barack Obama, who won 56 percent of their ballots compared with 49 percent of the men's vote. If the Republican Party hopes to win future elections, it knows it can't concede women to the Democrats, especially not with the top-heavy success of President Obama among African Americans and Hispanics. White men made up only *36 percent* of the electorate in 2008, far from enough to form a majority party. (During the 2008 campaign, when the Democratic nomination battle pitted a female candidate against a black one, news organizations asked the Census Bureau when white men stopped making up the majority in this country. The answer: They never were the majority. They've just always acted like they were.) Political realities put women in the enviable position of having both parties vie for their attention.

And the number of women in Congress continues to grow. Since the 2008 election, seventeen women now belong to the "most exclusive club in America," the U.S. Senate. And seventy-five women were elected as voting members of the House of Representatives, delighting my mother, who had brought the number of congresswomen up to a mere sixteen when she won her special election in March 1973. She's especially pleased with the ascendance of a woman she helped to mentor, Nancy Pelosi, to Speaker of the House of Representatives. As the highest-ranking elected woman in American history, Pelosi holds a constitutional office, not just a political one, and stands after the vice president in the line of succession to the presidency. Her election as Speaker in 2007 marked a moment that Pelosi recognized as she accepted the gavel, surrounded by the children who flock to the floor of the House of Representatives on the day a parent is sworn in: "This is an historic moment—for the Congress, and for the women of this country. . . . For our daughters and granddaughters, today we have broken the marble ceiling." Women have now knocked over every political barrier except president and vice president.

One of the last to fall before Speaker of the House was state attorney general. Voters just didn't seem ready to elect a woman as the chief law enforcement officer. Finally, in 1984, Arlene Violet, a Republican woman in Rhode Island, leaped that hurdle. I was terribly interested in what had happened in the smallest state to give it the courage to elect "General Violet." Then I discovered that Arlene Violet had been a nun, and though voters might not be comfortable turning over law enforcement to a woman, they had no problem putting a nun in charge of disciplining the society. After she left office, General Violet became a radio talk show host, another place a former nun could shine.

So what about a woman president? Why have other countries been able to break that barrier and we have not? I think the answer lies in the difference between the parliamentary and presidential systems. In a parliamentary system a woman can become head of her party and then head of the government if her party gets elected. That's a somewhat easier task than the singular one assigned to the American presidential candidate. Voters tend to cast the ballot for that office based on a gut-check—do I trust the candidate's judgment enough that I think he'll do the right thing regardless of what issue might arise? Or do I at least trust him more than the other guy (and it's still only guys)? It's a very personal vote. And one that can be tough for a woman. The 2008 election underlined that fact. During the campaign almost three-quarters of white voters told *Los Angeles Times* pollsters that they thought the country was ready for a black president, while fewer than two-thirds said the same about a woman. And things that were said about the women running, the blatant sexism in the media and among the late-night comedians about New York senator Hillary Clinton, deeply depressed me. And the abuse of Alaska governor Sarah Palin, the Republican nominee for vice president, was particularly discouraging.

Whether you agree or disagree with either of those women is not the point. The point is that they were treated very differently from men. The words used to describe them—even the ones used in public like *shrill* or *aggressive* or *ambitious*—were words that would never have been used negatively about a man. And a man would never have been asked about who would take care of the children. It just wouldn't happen. Longtime Democratic congresswoman and erstwhile presidential candidate Pat Schroeder constantly complained about the double standard applied to female versus male office seekers when she came to Congress with small children in the early 1970s. When she was asked how she could be both a congresswoman and a mother, she would raise hackles with her response: "I have a brain and a uterus, and they both work." Women running for office in recent years thought that had begun to change. "In previous years, when I have run for office, I always had to overcome being a woman," Texas senator Kay Bailey Hutchison said after a recent election, but she saw some improvement. "All

I've ever wanted was an equal chance to make my case, and I think we're getting to that point—and that's the victory."

But it's not enough of a victory. Until a woman is elected president, girls growing up in this country will see limits on what they can accomplish. Sure, it's bound to happen sooner or later. I just want it to be sooner. Until Hillary Clinton came close to snaring the nomination, I always believed that the first woman president was likely to be a vice president who came to office because of the misfortune—natural or otherwise—of a male president. That still might be the case. As long as we don't organize to do him in, that's okay with me.

Human Rights

Champion

▦　　▦　　▦

"IN THIS ROLE YOU ALWAYS WONDER IF YOU'RE UNDER-stood at all when you see the characterization that certainly your political opponents make of you . . . but on the other hand that's part of politics and certainly American politics. And you know when you get in the race, any race here for politics, that that's going to happen." That was First Lady Laura Bush's answer to a BBC reporter's question about whether her husband was misunderstood. I don't know if she privately handled the criticism so sanguinely, but she certainly understood the pitfalls as well as the privileges of occupying the White House. It's an understanding that's not always come easily to the women, and it's still only *women,* who have occupied that strange but important position as presidential spouse. Americans have always had a fascination with First Ladies—those unelected and unfireable women who have no official role but still wield tremendous influence over the man who has for the better part of a century been the most powerful person in the world.

Martha Washington knew that all eyes were on her when she arrived in the temporary first capital city of New York, so she eschewed her preferred silks and satins in favor of homespun when she stepped off the barge that carried her across the Hudson River to greet the gathered throngs. Her every move was so watched by the public that she came to describe her job as "Chief State Prisoner," and she didn't even live in the prison itself—the White House. It was Abigail Adams who famously took up residence in the unfinished "Executive Mansion," and she serves as a prime example of a First Lady who could not shake off the criticism—could not accept the fact, as Laura Bush did, that it comes with the territory. The second president's wife was a fascinating figure in the formation of our country and a useful political adviser to her husband, John, for most of his career. But she could never handle the attacks, either by political opponents or the press. To be sure, the opposition, led by Adams's own vice president, Thomas Jefferson, *was* vicious, but it would have worked better for John Adams if Abigail could have adopted Laura Bush's philosophical approach. Instead she railed against the "batteries of abuse and scurrility" of the press. Her desire to silence her husband's opponents led the First Lady to push John hard to support the Alien and Sedition Acts. "Nothing will have an effect until Congress pass a Sedition Bill, which I presume they will do before they rise," she wrote to her sister. "I wish the laws of our country were competent to punish the stirrer up of sedition, the writer and printer of base and unfounded calumny." The passage of those politically unpalatable laws, which sent opposition newspapermen to jail for criticizing the president, went a long way toward the defeat of John Adams after only one term.

Abigail Adams was an outspoken and sometimes outrageously partisan First Lady (one member of the opposing party called her "Mrs. President, not of the United States but of a faction"), but she was far from unique in her assertiveness. I've spent a good deal of time and energy over the last several years trying to dispel the myth that presidents' wives sat around tending to the tatting until Eleanor Roosevelt came along, and that after her Hillary Clinton, and maybe Rosalynn Carter, were the only ones who played public roles. Nothing could be further from the truth. Starting with Martha Washington, who lobbied for pensions for veterans of the Revolution, men she had gotten to know over eight long years of war, most First Ladies have wielded considerable power as their husbands' counselors and cocampaigners. ("Mrs. Madison saved the administration of her husband," James G. Blaine wrote of Dolley Madison. "But for her DeWitt Clinton would have been chosen president in 1812.") Laura Bush knew that history and was amused and somewhat annoyed when her husband was first elected and she was repeatedly asked, "Are you going to be Barbara Bush or Hillary Clinton?" Though she recalled those questions with a laugh at a White House session with reporters and historians as her husband's term came to a close, Mrs. Bush added, "Our First Ladies are much more complicated than they ever get treated in the media. And I think what happens is a story goes up around them, a myth that people stick to, for all of the coverage of them forever after." Her own least favorite? "This morning I read in the newspaper that I was prim. What is that? I think that's a librarian."

Even so, this librarian admits that it took her a while to realize the power of her position ("I can't believe I was so dense"). But it didn't take her long to learn that when she spoke people listened, and she started speaking out more and more—on the plight of women in Afghanistan, on HIV/AIDS, on literacy, on heart disease, on Burma. And while she was speaking she was doing—establishing the National Book Festival, luring more than a hundred thousand people to the National Mall every year to listen to authors and buy books, meeting with women in the Middle East to bring the subject of breast cancer out into the open, blogging from Africa about its burdens and beauties, traveling three times to Afghanistan to shore up support for women and girls in that country. And Laura Bush came to realize that her doing and talking mattered: "Every time I spoke out about something, even heart disease, I would be surprised again at how many people heard me. And I often used Lady Bird Johnson's quote about the First Lady has a podium and while she was here, she said, 'I've decided to use it.' And Lady Bird certainly did." Laura Bush remembers an encounter with a saleswoman in a department store in Texas responding to her plea for the women of Afghanistan, which she made as the first presidential spouse to substitute for her husband on his weekly radio address. As she told Fox News: "That's when I realized I had a podium. And did I act upon it that much? Then, probably not . . . I grew in both my realization that I had a podium but also in my expertise about some international issues that I didn't come to the White House with."

What Laura Bush did come to the White House with was more knowledge about the historic mansion itself than any of her predecessors, since she had spent a good deal of time there with her mother- and father-in-law. More important, she brought a solid sense of self plus her experience as the First Lady of Texas. In that job she focused on health and education and created the Texas Book Festival, allowing the state to participate in her lifelong love affair with books. When she first arrived in Washington, she took on similar causes—causes born out of her own life experiences as a teacher, librarian, and daughter of a breast cancer survivor. She brought controversial scholars to the White House to discuss the writings of prominent American authors, convinced the Librarian of Congress to create the National Book Festival, and convened a conference on early childhood cognitive development. Mrs. Bush was on her way to Capitol Hill to testify about the findings of that conference before the Senate Education Committee (how did she get the reputation of being a Harriet Homebody?) when the second plane crashed into the World Trade Center on September 11, 2001. Sitting in the office of the man who was the very face of the political opposition—Senator Ted Kennedy—the First Lady worked the phones to locate her husband, children, and mother, and then she and Kennedy went before the waiting cameras, voicing their support for the people of New York and attempting to calm the nation. "You take the measure of a person at a time like that," Kennedy later told *Time* magazine. "She is steady, assured, elegant." Laura Bush also became a passionate promoter of the rights of women and girls in Afghanistan, the country where the terrorists who attacked America had trained and where their leader, Osama bin Laden, was believed to be hiding.

Two months after September 11, and six weeks after the United States and the United Kingdom invaded Afghanistan to overthrow the regime that harbored and sponsored terrorists, Laura Bush broadcast the first presidential radio address delivered by someone other than a president. It was a strong denunciation of the Taliban's treatment of women. "All of us have an obligation to speak out," she insisted. "The fight against terrorism is also a fight for the rights and dignity of women." It was after those words went out to the world that Laura Bush realized her voice could rally others to action. So she journeyed to Africa to speak out on HIV/AIDS and worked with her husband to establish PEPFAR—the President's Emergency Plan for AIDS Relief—one of the true successes of the Bush administration. It was established in 2003, when fifty thousand people in sub-Saharan Africa received treatment for AIDS, and by the time the Bushes left office, more than 2 million people in that area were getting treated, more than 10 million in the fifteen focus countries. She joined with the president and members of Congress to fight malaria, announcing in 2006 the Malaria Communities Program to combat the spread of the disease in Africa. She assembled groups of women in Saudi Arabia, Kuwait, Jordan, and the United Arab Emirates to break the deadly taboo on talking about breast cancer. If no one discusses the disease, no one knows the importance of early detection, and so 80 percent of the women diagnosed with breast cancer in some Middle Eastern countries die of it. Here at home it is heart disease that is killing women at an alarming rate—more than all cancers combined—so she took on that cause as well, organizing a First Ladies Red Dress exhibit, and once again taking her husband's place before the microphones in February 2008, designated as "American Heart Month," to tell women some of the warning signs of heart attacks and urge them to adopt healthier lifestyles.

As her understanding of the power of her presence increased, Laura Bush took on more—going time and again to the Katrina-ravaged Gulf Coast, listening to the grievances of those left homeless and hostile by the hurricane, and leaving behind libraries full of books for schoolchildren. As America's chief public diplomat she traveled the globe—to seventy-six countries—promoting AIDS awareness and treatment, antimalaria programs, girls' education, women's economic initiatives, and she circled back to Afghanistan, working with the schools, with women entrepreneurs, goading that government to remember the nation's women and girls, while making sure Americans did as well. One of her last public events before the Christmas season took over the White House at the end of George Bush's term was a teleconference with the U.S.-Afghan Women's Council, established by the presidents of the two countries to promote the interests of women in Afghanistan. Though it was housed initially in the State Department, Laura Bush managed to ensure its continuation in the next administration by working to move the organization out of government and into Georgetown University.

But for all her passion and commitment to the causes she worked on—health, education, literacy, libraries, the book festival, and the advancement of women—they could all in one way or another be pigeonholed as "women's issues," something everyone's mother, or perhaps a former elementary school teacher and librarian, might have taken on. Not so Laura Bush's firm opposition to the generals governing Burma. A somewhat fierce First Lady startled the White House press corps when she chose to go to the briefing room herself rather than allow a staff member to address the media after a devastating cyclone hit Burma in May 2008. The facts that the state-run media had not warned the populace of the approaching cyclone, that the military government was not allowing aid into the country, and that the generals were still planning to hold a sham election could not go unnoticed and uncriticized, in the view of Laura Bush, who was about to leave Washington for her daughter's wedding. So she herself stood at the lectern, knowing that the shock of seeing the president's wife there would mean the press paid attention when she attacked the constitutional referendum scheduled by the junta leaders who "orchestrated this vote to give false legitimacy to their continued rule." There was nothing prim about this lady as she flatly laid out the charges: "The constitution would prohibit democracy activists who are current or former political prisoners, including Aung San Suu Kyi, from taking office. To ensure their constitution becomes law the regime has been intimidating voters and using force against dissidents. Public gatherings have been banned and printed materials may not be distributed without governmental approval." Why, Laura Bush was asked that day, had she broken precedent and come herself to the briefing room? What was she doing there? She stated simply that she wanted "the world to pay attention to the people of Burma, and for the world to put pressure on the military regime." Here was a First Lady, standing in the White House pressroom, unapologetically calling for the overthrow of a government: "The response to the cyclone is just the most recent example of the junta's failure to meet its people's basic needs. The regime has dismantled systems of agriculture, education, and health care. This once wealthy nation now has the lowest per capita GDP in Southeast Asia."

Months later when I asked her why she took that somewhat dramatic step, why show up herself in the pressroom, she said, "I did know that would be the most effective." No longer "dense," to use her own self-deprecating term, it was now crystal clear to Laura Bush that her voice carried clout. Her appearance in the pressroom was perhaps the most unusual step the First Lady had taken in her determination to bring the plight of the people of Burma to the attention of the world, but it was hardly the first. She had been speaking out about the situation in that nation for years—ever since a relative working in the field of human rights had brought to her attention the story of Aung San Suu Kyi—the Nobel Peace Prize–winning woman who had been elected prime minister in 1990, though the military dictators had placed her under house arrest. Reading Suu Kyi's book led Laura Bush to learn more about the regime holding the country hostage—and she didn't like what she learned. "Burma used to have one of the very best economies in Asia; now it's the worst. And they're a very, very rich country—rich in natural resources—and the military regime has used those resources for their own benefit and is literally stripping the country of its patrimony," she told Charlie Rose in one of her many interviews on the subject.

In September 2006, taking advantage of the publicity surrounding the convening of the UN General Assembly, she pulled together a roundtable on Burma, starting a lobbying campaign to get the subject onto the Security Council agenda. In June 2007, on Aung San Suu Kyi's sixty-second birthday, she penned an editorial for the *Wall Street Journal* where she again directly challenged Burma's military leaders: "The regime's abuses have spawned more than 500,000 internally displaced persons and sent hundreds of thousands fleeing the country. Children are pressed into service as laborers, and reports indicate that the rape of girls is commonplace." She pressed the U.S. Congress to enact sanctions against the generals, called on the international community to step up its pressure on behalf of dissidents, and announced that she would meet later that day with the UN special envoy to Burma "to discuss how the international community can hold the generals to account." She made contact with human rights activists working on the Thai-Burmese border and counted on them to keep her up to date on what was happening there.

And then she pulled out the most powerful weapon in

any First Lady's quiver—the ability to influence her husband. During the so-called Saffron Revolution in September 2007, when Buddhist monks joined others in rising up against the regime, George Bush focused on Burma in his address to the United Nations: "The ruling junta remains unyielding, yet the people's desire for freedom is unmistakable. This morning, I'm announcing a series of steps to help bring peaceful change to Burma. The United States will tighten economic sanctions on the leaders of the regime and their financial backers. . . . And I urge the United Nations and all nations to use their diplomatic and economic leverage to help the Burmese people reclaim their freedom." No sooner were the words out of the president's mouth, his wife later remembered, "and we immediately get an e-mail from the Thai border." One of the activists she had been working with was thrilled. "What the American president says . . . immediately is around the world."

For all the excitement of the dissidents, however, and despite the success in convincing the Security Council to place Burma on its agenda, the generals there brutally cracked down on the Buddhist monks and other demonstrators. Laura Bush responded with a white-hot editorial to the *Wall Street Journal:* "People everywhere know about the regime's atrocities. They are disgusted by the junta's abuses of human rights. This swelling outrage presents the generals with an urgent choice: Be part of Burma's peaceful transition to democracy, or get out of the way for a government of the Burmese people's choosing." She revealed that the secretary general of the United Nations had called *her* to announce that he was sending the UN special envoy to Burma back to the region.

The generals, of course, did not get out of the way. They instead attempted to lend themselves legitimacy through the referendum the First Lady had so vehemently denounced from the White House pressroom. But Mrs. Bush was not daunted. In a show of her continued solidarity with the human rights cause, she made the difficult trip to the Thai-Burmese border where she met with refugees from the regime and visited a health clinic run by a woman known as the "Mother Teresa of Burma." On her way to the Olympic Games in China, Mrs. Bush took the opportunity to single out that country for some pressure from the president's wife: "We urge the Chinese to do what other countries have done—to sanction, to put a financial squeeze on the Burmese generals."

Laura Bush left public office with the Burmese generals still firmly in place, but she intends to keep up the campaign to remove them, using whatever power she possesses as a former First Lady. She will work with her husband to create a Freedom Institute as part of his library, and through it, "I'll be able to continue to work with Burma and with Afghanistan. It will be a vehicle for me to do what I've done," Mrs. Bush told that gathering of historians and journalists she met with at the White House a couple of months before her term ended. And she continues to work with the UN to promote literacy, particularly for the two-thirds of the 700 million illiterate people in the world who are women. Still, she knows her voice is not as loud outside of the White House as in it. "When the First Lady is interested, all the wheels are greased a lot faster. You really can call attention to things that the general public may not pay that much attention to, or members of Congress may not pay that much attention to." And so she did—for the benefit of the sick, uneducated, repressed, and abused—especially those who are women—of the world.

A U N T

"AUNTS ARE GREAT," CHIRPED MY THEN SEVEN-YEAR-OLD
niece one day when we were on an outing years ago. The
proximate cause of this utterly satisfying statement was a
gummy dinosaur just purchased by me at the Museum of
Natural History. It was at the end of a morning of many ad-
ventures, including subway rides, a visit to the new exhibition, and the offer that she and her twin sister could buy any
"little" thing they wanted at the museum store. For me, it
was a special time spent with two fascinating characters
whose behavior is not my responsibility. For them, it was a
chance to command my undivided attention, to be blissfully
"spoiled." A few weeks later, it was a great-niece's turn. She
had just turned four and I had promised her, as my godchild,

a day with just the two of us. No big sister, no baby brother. Just us. For this act of true friendship, as far as she was concerned, I was regularly rewarded with the most scrumptious of hugs and referred to as her "fairy godmother." Those little girls are now teenagers. The twins are off to college, the godchild is in high school. And days spent with them growing up have been some of my most enjoyable times. A relationship to an adult not your parent can be one of the best in life. Aunts, uncles, grandparents, great-aunts and -uncles, courtesy aunts and uncles—all made such a difference in my life, and in the lives of my own children. Now I find that the same is true in the other direction—that nieces and nephews, great-nieces and -nephews, and friends' children make my life richer and fuller. And now I am blessed with the great joy of grandchildren. Six of them, praise the Lord. And of course, one is more perfect than the next.

When I was growing up we lived part of the year in New Orleans, part of the year in Washington, so it had the feel of a somewhat schizophrenic childhood. In Louisiana, I was surrounded by family. My mother was an only child, but her mother sometimes lived next door with two of her sisters and their mother. Six blocks away was my mother's first cousin Shingo, not an actual aunt but considered one, what we call a "tante." Her daughters were just on either side of me in age. Though I found my own house fascinating with its mix of politicos from all parts of town and every ethnic background, it was sometimes a relief to skip the six safe blocks to a world with backyard swings and midday snacks. I loved stuffing envelopes at our dining room table with the campaign volunteers; it made me feel wonderfully competent to be able to fold the election flyers with the best of them. And I listened avidly to all the conversation about issues and intrigue. But it was also nice to listen as Shingo read children's stories, to go from tales of huge corruption to ones about high cockalorum. During one really rough campaign, even though her house was under construction and there was a new baby, I moved in with Shingo for most of the summer.

Various other relatives were always around. On any given night at my great-aunt Rowena's next door, twelve to fourteen people would gather around the dinner table, all related to me in some way that they would carefully explain if I couldn't get out of the way fast enough. Sometimes I would make the mistake of asking my mother or grandmother who some "stranger" was. That would evoke the lengthy genealogical discourse that southern families so love. My children correctly accuse me of the same sin.

My father's mother and father, about an hour and a half away on the Mississippi Gulf Coast, had a house on a big family compound, along with several of their children. In the summer I would spend weeks at a time there, going from one house to the next, but mainly staying with my aunt Tootsie who had seven children of her own and didn't seem to mind a few more. My aunts and my grandmother would tell my sister, brother, our cousins, and me stories of their childhood, and my father's. We loved to listen to any tales that portrayed him as a less than ideal child. His sisters were happy to lovingly oblige. Several of my cousins who are my contemporaries built houses on the property and it was wonderful fun to go back and tell one another's kids about all the outlaw things we did, like sneaking out to the beach at night or smoking under the bayou bridge. But then Hurricane Katrina hit and wiped out all their homes. The property, called Boggsdale, which had been in the family since just after the Civil War, was completely ravaged by wind and water. With all my cousins' homes plus my aunt's and my uncle's completely destroyed, with nothing recognizable left on the land, my aunt Tootsie, who had rebuilt after Camille, and after another big hurricane in 1947, decided at age ninety that she wasn't going to do it again. But, with pluck and perseverance, she and the rest of the family have settled into cozy homes farther away from the water but still close to one another. And though it's sad to visit the forsaken property that teemed with activity all of my life, it's wonderful that everyone is still there and together, including my aunt Tootsie who, as of this writing, is a vigorous ninety-three.

If our time in Louisiana and Mississippi was spent surrounded by family when we were kids, in Washington it was our parents' friends and, later, our friends' parents who were the meaningful grown-ups in our lives (other than our teachers and the housekeeper who ruled us). Because so many people move to the capital from someplace else, friends often become family in Washington even more so than in other places. And I think my parents' friends had grown especially close during World War II, when many of the men were away and the women banded together to pool the ration coupons and provide the moral support. We lived in a neighborhood where we were in and out of one another's houses, and someone else's mother was just as likely to take care of you as your own. My "aunt" Lizzie had the surest hand with the scissors, so she had the task of trimming my bangs and hemming my skirts. As we grew older, nearly all of my friends' grandmothers moved in with them. They would often help us with the costumes and cookies for school plays and bake sales, regaling us with stories of "the olden days" while we stitched and stirred.

At a party my parents gave for Lynda Johnson's wedding, President Johnson talked about how important it was for him to have befriended his father's friends and how important it was for his children to know his friends. It was a lovely sentiment, but it's the mothers and daughters whose friendships have lasted. Until she died Mrs. Johnson and my mother took vacations together, and Lynda and I have inherited their friendship. Lynda's daughter, Lucinda, and my Becca are buddies, but Lucinda was an even better friend of my sister, Barbara, a "tante" to her. And she feels close to my mother as well.

The men in this universe of adults often charmed and delighted us, but they were mostly drop-ins on our lives. It was the women we spent time with, it was from them that we learned about other generations, about how things used to be, and how things would forever be. My mother's mother and aunts were quite a group. My mother refers to them as flappers, but by the time I knew them well that era had passed. When I first became conscious of this sisterhood, each was on her second husband. For a while three of them and a half sister, plus my mother, were all married to men whose last names began with *B*. My mother loves to tell the story of the *B* handkerchiefs, given one Christmas by one of my great-aunts to my great-uncle Hewitt Bouanchaud. His wife, my great-aunt Eustatia, oohed and aahed over them and then quickly disappeared them to be rewrapped for the next Christmas and passed on to my great-aunt Frosty Black-shear's husband. Well, the same thing happened again, with each wife wrapping the handkerchiefs on each successive year until they went all the way around the family. Finally, they ended up in Hewitt's pile again. Much to the horror of the women, he declared, "These handkerchiefs have been given to every man in the family, starting with me. This year I'm keeping them." And he proceeded to stuff them in his pocket out of reach of Eustatia. It wasn't easy to get out of Eustatia's reach. She was a fun-loving, piano-playing presence. She composed ragtime songs that she accented with the *rat-a-tat* of her long fingernails on the keyboard.

One tune involved her stamping out a couple of chords with her foot and then banging out the finale with her rear end on the ivories.

Then the second husbands all died and the great-aunts set off in active pursuit of husbands number three. (Only my grandmother succeeded in this quest.) Their attempts to "vamp" men were something to behold, and they would bring us in on the fabulous plots. What an unimaginable treat! I thought the women were ancient, of course. Now I realize that in the 1950s, the years I was in school and living at home, they were in their fifties and early sixties. But age did not wither their attempts to find men. By the time I got married they were in their seventies and my grandmother's third husband had died. The sisters arrived for the wedding festivities and immediately accosted my twenty-three-year-old groom. "We hear you have two widowed grandfathers," my aunt Eustatia queried. "Why, yes," Steven somewhat bemusedly confirmed. "Is either of them creaky?" came the next question. Steven allowed as how one was creakier than the other. "Well, Co has first pick," said Eustatia to my now astonished about-to-be-mate. "After all, her granddaughter found you and they are your grandfathers. I never cut in on Co's men." Neither my grandmother, Corinne, nor my great-aunt Eustatia walked away with a new groom from my wedding, but that was due to no lack of effort on their parts.

Among the four sisters, though they wed nine husbands, they only had two children—my mother and my cousin

Dinky, my godmother. So Dinky's kids, who were all younger than we were, and Barbara and Tommy and I were the community grandchildren. The women took us to movies our parents would have never allowed, drove us down Bourbon Street to see their sister Frosty who lived there, and let us peek in the doors of the strip joints on the way. (When my kids were small, my mother moved into that Bourbon Street house and I used to jokingly chant, "Over the hills and through the woods to grandmother's house we go," as we tripped our way past the strippers and the other neighbors.) When my grandmother and her sisters were middle-aged, it was a great boon to be their only family. Then Dinky died very young. And it was hard on my mother to be the only child of four women as they grew old and died. By then, my generation was off starting families of our own.

My great-grandmother enjoyed the whole commotion of her daughter's household immensely, though she didn't participate in the vamping schemes. Instead, she took her pleasures in card games and at the racetrack. I remember once when "Rets" was in her nineties, my sister dragged a date to visit her in the hospital where she was fighting pneumonia. "Poor dear," sympathized the young man, whoever he was, "it's so easy to get sick at her age." "You'd have pneumonia too," Barbara shot back, "if you had spent all day at the races in the rain." When they got to the hospital, all my great-grandmother could talk about was the fact that her daughter Eustatia, "the wretch," had won the daily double.

When she was about fifteen years old and dating my brother, my sister-in-law, Barbara (yes, it's confusing, two Barbaras, my sister and sister-in-law, but you must admit the rest of the names are interesting), went dutifully to visit Rets, who had the flu. Barbara crept into the room, where the little old lady was sitting up in a giant four-poster bed covered by a crocheted afghan. How sweet, the teenager thought, she must be reading the Bible. On closer look she saw the title, *Return to Peyton Place*. Years later, Barbara and Tommy's daughter, Elizabeth, who had only seen her great-great-grandmother in bed, asked, "Does Rets have legs?"

My children haven't been blessed with the same sorts of characters entertaining them along the road to adulthood, but they have had a devoted group of family members and friends who have taken a keen interest in them, and for whom they are now sharing responsibility. My daughter, Rebecca, learned about that responsibility at a young age when she went to Princeton University, partly to be near her aunt Barbara, the closest any of our generation came to genuine "character" status. As the mother of three boys, my sister lusted after a daughter, and readily adopted Becca as her own. The night before school started we were staying at Barbara's house getting ready for a farewell-to-our-daughter dinner. Becca discovered a run in her stockings and went knocking on her aunt's bedroom door, asking to borrow a pair. "I've been waiting all my life for this moment," Barbara announced with much fanfare.

The two of them had a great time together Rebecca's freshman year. Barbara was running for governor and Becca, who at the age of nine had worked in one of my mother's congressional races, campaigned across the state. She and her aunt were a formidable duo, as Barbara called on her niece to make speeches, or shake hundreds of hands. Years earlier, when our parents moved into a smaller house in New Orleans, they sent the dining room table to Princeton, so it was back in use as campaign central. Becca was disappointed but not surprised when Barbara lost the primary, and sophomore year started as a more leisurely time when aunt and niece could kick back and enjoy spare moments together. But in October Barbara was diagnosed with incurable cancer, and Becca found herself in a different role. At first it was diversion that was necessary, then errand running and filling in at public events, then helping put together a book of Barbara's poems for publication. ("Becca, I wrote a poem about Christmas. I think I wrote it on a grocery bag and filed it at the mayor's office. It's not in the front of the office, it's in the back, where I keep the borough budget.") Then it was caretaking.

When Rebecca went to England over the summer before her junior year, she traveled with much trepidation about her aunt. But Barbara's boys were home and needed their own time with their mother. As junior year began, my sister's condition worsened considerably and my daughter became her primary nurse. Barbara felt safe with Becca, se-cure in her niece's arms when she needed help to the bath-room, unembarrassed in a way she was not even with her husband. While it was not the way most juniors in college spend their time, it was an experience Becca wouldn't trade for anything. At Barbara's request, Becca sang at her funeral, and I joined her in harmony. And then, after the funeral, after the hundreds of mourners had gone back to their lives, it was Becca who was left in Princeton, bereft of her aunt but still liable for her legacy. So she would go to the various banquets and benefits, accepting awards in Barbara's name, extolling her aunt's virtues, along with those of whatever group sought recognition.

As we grow older, I see the next generation taking on the blessings and burdens of the community of aunts. When I first wrote this book, my niece, Elizabeth, despite the rigors of raising three children while holding down a demanding full-time job, was already at a stage in her life when we could count on her to show up unbidden when anyone was in need. And my daughter was delightedly playing the role of tante to all of the little kids. Her twin cousins had visited her when she lived in Philadelphia as a young single woman, and all of the little girl relatives were flower girls at her wedding. Now Elizabeth and Rebecca have moved into the caretaking roles, keeping their protective eyes on the older generations; the "little girl relatives" have moved into the teenage tante positions, entertaining the little kids, including Becca's boys.

What joy these relationships provide! Most of us know how important friends and family are, but it always comes home to us with force at times of great upheaval—births, deaths, moves, marriages. The year both of my children got married, they found themselves surrounded by circles of caring aunts and tantes. Almost all of their "real" aunts and uncles gave parties, welcoming the new young people into the family and introducing them to their friends. The cousins who had lived six blocks away in New Orleans when I was a little girl now live near us in suburban Washington. As they helped with houseguests and homecomings and provided endless hospitality, they also handed on the stories. Our childhood suddenly came alive again, just at the moment I was feeling like an over-the-hill mother of bride and groom.

And my friends—women I'd known over the years as a young wife and then mother, and friends from work who helped me through the growing-up years, trying to mute their giggles during the after-school phone calls ("Rebecca, you have an obligation to go to your piano lesson, you've made a commitment"; "Lee, stop picking on your sister")— all pitched in to make it perfect for my kids. Becca asked my friend Millie, a tante to her, to act in the role of rabbi. She wanted Judaism in the ceremony, but Judaism in a skirt. As I looked at the people gathered together at the weddings, including the people who would now be their families and their warm and welcoming friends, it struck me so strongly that this is what community is all about. A marriage is a formal entrance into the grown-up world, and these would be the people on hand to help in all the transitions involved. The women, I realized, would be there in the way they always have been. And now the "kids" are there for them.

SOLDIER

▨   ▨   ▨

FOR MANY YEARS ON THE WALL ABOVE MY DESK AT WORK
hung a facsimile copy of the discharge of one "Frank Deming" from the United States Army during the Civil War.
Reason for dismissal: "Because of her sex . . . being a female." That's the kind of wonderful present women I've
never met send me when we've just debated something on
television about women in the military. Over the years,
we've had a lot of those debates. The discharge paper of
"Frank Deming" is a perceptive viewer's way of informing
me that this is not even a slightly new discussion.

   With the country waging two wars over the last several
years, and well over two hundred thousand women in uniform, no one can escape the significant role women are

playing in the all-volunteer force as we watch moms in fatigues kissing their infants farewell. I must admit to some degree of discomfort looking at those pictures. It's unquestionable that the technology of war has changed so dramatically that brains matter as much as brawn. But the question of women in combat remains a thorny one for the politicians. Despite the insistence by military women that they will never achieve equal status if combat roles are denied them, and the protests of those who have been there that they are already exposed to the full dangers of warfare, women are still officially denied combat roles. More than a hundred uniformed women have lost their lives in Iraq and Afghanistan, but the brass insists that the public's not ready to accept the concept of women in body bags; also, women cannot be trusted to perform well in combat, and fighting men might make poor judgments in order to protect a romantic interest in the next foxhole. Women in the military tend to give rude responses to those arguments, and their degree of exasperation is understandable—if impolitic— since they have both their own experience and that of women in all of America's wars on their side.

As in so many other areas of female endeavor in the last generation or so, we tend to think that the idea of women on the battlefield is something brand-new under the sun. Now politicians honoring the military regularly refer to our "men and women in uniform." But the first time I remember hearing that term invoked repeatedly was during the congressional debate on the Persian Gulf War back in 1991. (As a reporter covering the debate, I was struck by this interesting bit of rhetoric, and then I realized that it was also the first time I had regularly heard the phrase "our men in the military." It had always been "our boys in Vietnam" or "our boys in Korea," leading me to the quite delightful observation that this was not the first time a woman had turned a boy into a man.)

There is now in Washington, in addition to the Vietnam Women's Memorial, the Women in Military Service for America Memorial, a museum dedicated to the women who served in every American conflict. But most people don't seem quite clear on what it is those women did. When the indefatigable General Wilma Vaught was rounding up supporters to build the memorial at the gateway to Arlington National Cemetery, there was even a commentary on NPR that such a monument was undeserved because it equated the lowly jobs of women during war with the heroic deeds of men. A little ignorance goes a long way. Even the most cursory reading reveals that women have been there since the Revolution, carrying the standards into battle, taking up the weapons of those who had fallen, braving the bullets to care for the wounded and dying, brazenly crossing enemy lines as couriers and scouts, daringly tricking ciphers and codes out of Redcoat and Rebel, Vichy leader and Vietcong.

Now that the National Park Service provides reenactments at some battlefield sites, more of us have become aware of the camp followers—the women who went to war with their husbands and sweethearts, doing the cooking and laundry. Many of them also joined the fray. Two well-known figures from the Revolutionary War, Molly Pitcher and Margaret Corbin, both took their husbands' places on the fields of battle, one at Monmouth, one at Fort Washington. Their heroic exploits have come down to us over the centuries through song and story—Molly "Pitcher," who was probably a woman named Mary Hays, got her nickname because she is supposed to have supplied water to thirsty soldiers and dropped her pitcher when her husband was hit, taking his place at the cannon—but verification comes through the much more mundane method of researching pension records and learning that these women received military retirement benefits. Margaret Corbin, who sustained three gunshot wounds, battled the bureaucracy until she received the full ration—including rum or whiskey—due her. She is the only Revolutionary War veteran reburied at West Point.

Another pensioner whose tales of derring-do are documented was Deborah Sampson, who disguised herself as a man, fought through the Revolution, though twice wounded, and was only found out when she went to the hospital with "brain fever." After the war she made a living entertaining crowds with her stirring speeches: "I threw off the soft habiliment of my sex, and assumed those of the warrior, already prepared for battle." You have the feeling life was never as exciting again. After she died, Congress awarded her husband survivor's benefits, declaring that Deborah's "sickness and suffering were occasioned by the wounds she received and the hardships she endured in defense of the country."

Then there were the spies. Spying seems to have taken on the status of women's work throughout the country's conflicts. Several from Revolutionary times—women with the sturdy names of Sybil Ludington, Deborah Champion, Lydia Barrington Darragh, Emily Geiger, and Susanna Bolling—risked their lives riding horses over many miles for several days, crossing rivers in the night, sneaking through enemy territory, swallowing rather than surrendering messages, all getting word to the American troops of British plans of attack.

We all know of Dolley Madison's courage in the face of British marauders in the War of 1812, how she saved vital government documents and the portrait of George Washington before escaping from the White House, where the soldiers added insult to injury by first sitting down to the meal she had prepared, before they set fire to her home. We've also read of the famous battles of the U.S.S. *Constitution* ("Old Ironsides"), but most of us don't know that a woman named Lucy Brewer claimed to be one of the sailors aboard, disguised as George Baker. The battle that gave victory to the United States in that war, a battle fought after the treaty was negotiated, was in my hometown of New Orleans, where we grew up hearing of the courage of the Ursuline nuns who collaborated with the American troops.

But it was in the Civil War that the necessity for women became clear. My friend Frank Deming seems to have been just one of a great many women who disguised themselves as men in order to fight. One, Jennie Hodgers, was only discovered when she moved into an old soldiers' home at the end of her life; another, a sergeant in General Rosecrans's ranks, had to confess to her sex when she gave birth to a baby. Other women went to war as the equivalent of mascots of regiments, pulling duty as pickets, scouts, and raiders. Several won decorations for their service; others received commissions in the regular army. And again, there was the full complement of spies. Among the best known was Harriet Tubman, who led a union colonel and several hundred black soldiers on a raid that freed eight hundred slaves. For her scouting and spying she was honored with a military funeral at the end of her long life. Then there was the Confederate Belle Boyd, who at the age of seventeen shot and killed a northern soldier for insulting her mother. She then went on to a colorful career as courier and spy, which earned her a commission as captain from Stonewall Jackson, and eventual banishment to Canada by the Union. Some women were less lucky—they landed in prison and were even executed for their devotion to duty as they saw it. They must have been doing something of great importance; otherwise, it wouldn't have merited the death penalty.

It was in far more "womanly" tasks, however, that the distaff side distinguished itself in the Civil War. Individual women like "Mother Bickerdyke" went foraging through the fields collecting linens and bandages and boiling them up in giant cauldrons until they were able to get military laundries going. And Annie Wittenmeyer, appalled at the military diet, stared down generals in order to establish wholesome kitchens in the hospitals. When these women faced opposition from the brass, they threatened to go to the press to expose the conditions of the fighting forces. But early in the war, it became clear that more than individual efforts were needed, that neither the Confederate nor the Union government was equipped to deal with huge numbers of soldiers going off to war. There was no Red Cross (something that was later remedied by another Civil War heroine, Clara Barton), no USO, no organization to feed, clothe, or nurse the vast armies called into service. Chaos ensued as families tried to get provisions willy-nilly to soldiers at the front. So Louisa Schuyler, a great-granddaughter of Alexander Hamilton, convened a mass meeting at Cooper Union in New York to organize for soldiers' relief. Out of that grew the U.S. Sanitary Commission, largely staffed by women volunteers who managed to supply the troops from community warehouses that they established all over the country. To raise money for their wares, women staged elaborate "sanitary fairs" in major cities where they auctioned off such items as the original Emancipation Proclamation. Over the course of the war the fairs brought in more than $25 million.

One of the things that interested me most as I learned

this history was how reluctant the commanders were to accept women as nurses. It came as a surprise to me that there had been no system for caring for the wounded before the Civil War. Apparently, fellow soldiers and camp followers had always done the nursing in the past. But as women saw the great need for their services to treat the ever-growing numbers of bodies filled with sickness and shrapnel, they started working, unbidden, in the hospitals. At first this caused great consternation, and the Confederate Congress ordered an investigation of the hospitals to see if women were doing any harm. The report revealed that the mortality rate in female-run hospitals was half that of those run by men. The Congress then passed laws giving women control of the hospitals, and gave "preference in all cases to females" in lower-level jobs, causing much grumbling by the men about "petticoat government." In the North, Dorothea Dix, a well-known crusader for the rights of the mentally ill, went to the acting surgeon general soon after the war began, to propose that she recruit a nursing corps of women volunteers. To answer the doctors' concerns that bringing women into the hospitals would cause sexual scandal, Dix agreed that "No woman under thirty years need apply to serve in government hospitals" and "All nurses are required to be very plain-looking women. Their dresses must be brown or black, with no bows, no curls, no jewelry and no hoopskirts." In addition, they were required to bring letters of recommendation from their pastors! The history books tell us that no scandals ensued, but a few nurses were transferred because of "impertinence" to surgeons.

It was in this role as nurses that the military began eventually to admit women officially into the ranks. Female nurses were recruited for the Spanish-American War at the end of the nineteenth century, and a permanent female nurse corps was established in law at the beginning of the twentieth: first the Army Nurse Corps in 1901, then the Navy Nurse Corps in 1908. In all, about twenty thousand of these women served in World War I, when the navy also established the "Yeomanettes" and the marines the "Marinettes," mostly for clerical work. After the war the services demobilized the almost thirteen thousand women enlistees.

By the time World War II was declared the women were ready. The Women's Voluntary Services started training ambulance drivers, first-aid workers, and mobile kitchen forces more than a year before Pearl Harbor. Congresswoman Edith Nourse Rogers steered through legislation establishing the Women's Army Auxiliary Corps, which allowed women to serve but gave them no military status and no benefits. That changed in 1943, when the "Auxiliary" was dropped and the WACs became official members of the armed forces. The navy equivalent—the WAVES (Women Accepted for Volunteer Emergency Service)—had been created by Congress a year earlier. In the course of the war one hundred forty thousand women served in the army, one hundred thousand in the navy, and another one hundred thousand went as Coast Guard personnel and Red Cross nurses. Even the marines learned they needed more than a few good men—twenty-three thousand women marines served between 1943 and 1945. The demand for nurses was such that Congresswoman Frances Bolton successfully passed into law creation of the Cadet Nurse Corps, where those who promised to serve the government's military or civilian needs were provided federal funds for nursing school. Still, the constant call for nurses was such that President Roosevelt asked Congress to draft nurses into the military. The measure passed the House and was still before the Senate when the war ended. And to think that much of the argument about the ill-fated Equal Rights Amendment was about the big taboo on drafting women! Not surprisingly, when the demand was great, the debate was not.

I remember as a little girl wanting to belong to the WAVES, and trying to devise a navy uniform out of my wardrobe. It was not long after World War II, and everyone's house had pictures of all the men in the family in uniform. My father had been in the navy, so of course, that was the branch I chose. As it turned out, I later went to Wellesley College, where former president Mildred McAfee Horton had been the first captain in charge of the WAVES. Colonel Oveta Culp Hobby, who commanded the WACs, was a prominent figure in 1950s Washington as a member of President Eisenhower's cabinet. Though I never met them, these were women of great stature in my girlhood, women to be admired and emulated.

There were also the Women Air Force Service Pilots (or WASP), who were the first women to fly military aircraft, ferrying every type of airplane to bases where they were needed. In a book of letters from women in the military in World War II, *We're in This War, Too,* the excitement of pilot Marion Stegeman of Athens, Georgia, sounds like that of any flyboy you've ever talked to. "Mother," she wrote during her training in Texas in 1943, "you haven't lived until you get way up there—all alone—just you and that big, beautiful plane humming under your control." When it became clear in the spring of 1944 that the Army Air Forces had a glut of pilots and the WASP were no longer deemed essential, Marion consulted her mother about whether she should resign and marry her fiancé. "How about a long letter of advice from you—and also please ask Aunt Heluiz and Grannie what they think." It might be a new set of questions for the women of the family, but she trusted their judgment. And so Marion Stegeman, eager to marry her marine, resigned. But many other women continued to serve, and risked enormous dangers: thirty-eight of them were killed in service. But when the program ended, former WASP Deanie Parrish later remembered, the women "packed their bags and paid their way back home. There were no GI benefits, no fringe benefits, and no dress parades—just the satisfaction of knowing they had done their duty and they had completed their mission." It took thirty-three years before Congress finally awarded these World War II pilots military status, and they never got the praise and pensions they deserved. But, as Deanie Parrish wrote to me, at least they will be able to be buried with an American flag draping their coffins. (My own mother spearheaded the congressional move to recognize the WASP, and she tells a funny story about getting cosponsors for the bill. One old-line Protestant male colleague said as he signed, "I don't know what your bill does, but there are so few of us WASPs left, could I sign on to it too?")

I finally met Deanie Parrish and several of her sister pilots in 2008 when the Women in Military Service for America Memorial opened a "Fly Girl" exhibit. These old ladies, all in military uniforms, still felt the thrill of flying. Here's Florence Reynolds: "I always wanted to fly. I thought everybody wanted to fly." Scotty Gough added, "If I had the money, I would have gladly paid the air force to let me fly those wonderful planes." Millicent Young recalled a refueling stop where the guy pumping the gas looked in the window and declared he should be flying the plane since he was a man. Her retort: "Honey, if you were, I'da noticed." As the crowd milled around before the opening of the exhibit, one of the women asked me why a young air force officer there was decorated with so many ribbons. When I answered, "Because she's a Thunderbird pilot," the WASP looked at one of her ex-colleagues and pronounced, "We could do that." The Thunderbirds fly advanced fighter aircraft in precision demonstrations around the world, and the first female pilot asked to join them, Nicole Malachowski, gives the WASP full credit for getting women behind the controls of military aircraft. "I am standing on your shoulders," she saluted them.

The letters from women who fought through World War II are some of the most affecting you would ever want to read. These women are so incredibly competent and unfailingly compassionate that I find my eyes filling with tears as I peer into their pasts. It also makes me angry that anyone would claim that they were in anything but the most essential and exposed positions. Here's a nurse writing her parents from Pearl Harbor: "The wounded started coming in 10 minutes after the first attack. . . . Then comes the second attack— We all fell face down on the wounded in the halls, O.R. and everywhere and heard the bombers directly over us. We had no helmets nor gas masks. . . . One of the soldiers who works for my ward saw me and so we shared helmets together. In the meantime the bombs were dropping all around us and when a 500 lb. bomb dropped about [censored] from the [censored] . . . then they were gone." And that, it goes without saying, was just the beginning.

Women in combat fatigues waded ashore for the North African invasion in 1942, arrived in Normandy on D-Day plus four in June 1944, and by July were in France in force. The stories of Red Cross workers landing in war zones and somehow setting up cheery cafés complete with curtains and coffee along with their trademark doughnuts never cease to amaze me. And then there are the agonizing letters from Anzio. "There is nothing to write about but the wounded," June Wandrey confided to her parents in June 1944. "We live down in the ground in sand-bagged, damp, smelly foxholes." Foxholes where they not only worked to make their patients whole but constantly battled to save them, and themselves, from strafing. There were flight nurses in the Pacific who would toil through the night keeping their charges alive in body and soul, and then rush to put on makeup before landing to fulfill regulations that nurses look attractive and fresh as hospital vessels hit the ground, regulations these women write about very matter-of-factly. They were women fighting constantly for normalcy in an insane world. There's the wonderfully refreshing letter of Billie Oliver, written from New Guinea a couple of weeks before her marriage, asking her parents, "Will you please get me a real sexy nightgown. You know, the kind a bride would wear. . . . After all, I will have to get married in uniform. I'd like to let my boy know he's got a woman, not a soldier."

He had, of course, a woman and a soldier. That's something these women learned about themselves. Army nurse Helen McKee wrote her parents from Italy right after VE Day about one boy for whom the war lasted just a few days too long—he had lost his arm and both eyes: "Of course, we are supposed to be accustomed to seeing handless arms, and your ears should be deaf to the groans of agony from these poor souls, but alas the two years of combat has not hardened the heart. . . . I don't think anyone felt closer, or shared the pain of these boys more than we, the A.N.C. Now we have finished our jobs, we've seen the war thru. We are tired and ready to come home." But for some there was still more to come. June Wandrey had left Italy and gone on to Germany. There, after the war in Europe was officially over, she found herself treating the victims of Dachau. "I'm on night duty with one hundred corpse-like patients," she wrote her parents in a horrifyingly vivid account. "God, where are you?"

It was a question asked in war in every century. And it was a question especially asked by women, who since the time of Lysistrata have been on record as ardent enemies of armed conflict. Public-opinion polling from its inception has shown women more opposed to war than men. And yet, ironically, wars have the effect of improving the economic lives of many women. So it was in the Civil War that women went to work in government agencies and arsenals. Southern women became shopkeepers and teachers in numbers that required the upgrading of women's education. And in World War II, 6 million women who had never worked outside the home joined the civilian labor force. African-American women moved from domestic work to factories. Half the rural black female labor force found jobs in the cities. Taking an editorial look at all this change, the *Minnesota Tribune* in August 1942 asked the questions "WACs and WAVES and women welders. . . . Where is it all going to end? . . . Is it hard to foresee after the boys come marching home and they marry these emancipated women, who is going to tend the babies in the next generation?" The answer, to no one's real surprise, turned out to be the women. But, despite all efforts to put the genie back in the bottle, the world for women would never be the same again. The campaign to send Rosie the Riveter home to the split-level ranch house largely succeeded. But women who had performed for this nation both overseas and on the home front knew what they had done and were proud of it. That generation of women raised the huge postwar baby boom and created all this modern confusion about a woman's place. No institution is more turned like a pretzel on that question—where should women be and what roles should they be playing?—than the military. Some women in reserve units have been called back to Iraq and Afghanistan two and three times, just like the men, and those women—medics, truck drivers, bomber pilots, navigators, tanker pilots, weapons officers, intelligence officers— are in harm's way every day, subject to being blown up, shot at, and, tragically, sexually assaulted by fellow soldiers. But they are by all accounts doing a first-rate job. Just ask Carolyn Schapper, a Virginia Army National Guard sergeant who participated in almost two hundred combat missions in Iraq; she told PBS's *NewsHour,* "Women are doing the same jobs as men, the majority of the time, and they're doing them very well." Still, the official ban against their going into combat, which exists in name more than in fact, keeps these women from rising to the highest ranks of their services.

But they're beginning to get close. In 2008 the army named its first female four-star general. At a standing-room-only "pinning" ceremony presided over by the secretary of defense, Ann Dunwoody told the cheering crowd, "How fortunate I [have] been to live a lifetime of firsts. And it's the army . . . that's given me that opportunity." The army was in her blood—with some member of the Dunwoody family serving in every war since the Revolution and her brother, father, grandfather, and great-grandfather graduates of West Point. When Ann Dunwoody and her sister, one of the army's first helicopter pilots, went to college, girls couldn't go to the military academy, Army Chief of Staff General George Casey reminded the audience at the ceremony, and, he added, Dunwoody also couldn't join the regular army when she signed up right out of college. She came in as a WAC before President Carter integrated women into the army. In 1975, the year Dunwoody signed up for her life's work, General Casey continued with a laugh, a survey of army personnel asked what was the most appropriate job for a woman in the army. The answer from 98 percent of the respondents? Cook. But that didn't stop Ann Dunwoody: "I couldn't believe they were going to pay me to jump out of airplanes," she told the crowd just after her fourth star was pinned to her shoulders. And she loved doing it, parachuting into war zones as she rose to become, according to Casey, the army's premier logistician. As the new head of the Materiel Command, Dunwoody told her admirers, "And while I know that I may be the first woman to achieve this honor, I know with certainty I won't be the last." Since her nomination for a fourth star earlier in the year, General Dunwoody said she had heard from hundreds of people: "I heard from men and women. . . . I heard from moms and dads who see this promotion as a beacon of hope for their own daughters. . . . I've heard from women veterans of all wars."

I was with some of those women veterans that day—it was the day the "Fly Girl" exhibit opened at the Women in Military Service for America Memorial—and they could barely contain their excitement. Vietnam War veteran Wilma Vaught, who conceived of the museum that pays tribute to military women and has worked relentlessly to raise the funds for it, came into the air force in 1957, when women were prohibited from reaching the rank of general or admiral. It took an act of Congress to correct that injustice. One of the most highly decorated women in the U.S. military, Brigadier General Vaught, when she retired in 1985, was one of seven female generals in all of the armed forces. When General Dunwoody's promotion was announced, she was one of fifty-seven admirals and generals. About 5 percent of the army's generals are female, compared with 14 percent of the total force, but only four serve above the one-star rank of brigadier general. The prohibition on women in combat will have to be lifted before those numbers will improve.

But Ann Dunwoody knows what women are doing in to-day's wars; her own niece is a fighter pilot who's flown missions over Afghanistan. She knows they're not protected by the ban, they're just constricted by it. So when she says that she knows "with certainty" that she won't be the last female four-star general, it's because she will be pulling her sisters along and pushing the army to promote them for doing their jobs well regardless of their sex. That's all these military women say they're after, and it's something Defense Secretary Robert Gates implicitly recognized at Dunwoody's ceremony: "History will no doubt take note of her achievement in breaking through this final 'brass ceiling' to pin on a fourth star. But she would rather be known—and remembered—first and foremost, as a U.S. Army soldier." And be treated like any other U.S. Army soldier. That's what women have wanted in every war.

E DUCATION R EFORMER

■   ■   ■

"I LOVE MY JOB. I CAN THINK OF NOTHING BETTER TO DO
every day than to make sure that the forty-six thousand kids
in this district get the education they deserve, finally." Michelle Rhee's enthusiasm is somewhat remarkable on two
counts—first, that she could love a job where her goals have
been frustrated and she gets yelled at constantly for trying
to achieve them, and second, that she believes she actually
can ensure quality education for the children of the nation's
capital. But this thirty-eight-year-old chancellor of the Washington, D.C., public schools, who was praised by both the
Democratic and Republican candidates for president during
a 2008 debate, is determined to take action to support her

words—to insist that the kids of the capital city get a decent education.

In 2007 when the new young mayor Adrian Fenty picked Rhee as the seventh person to head the D.C. schools in ten years, there was a good bit of head shaking over the choice. The Korean-American woman with no experience in managing a bureaucracy would be dealing with a school population that is 85 percent African American. But Rhee, who had started and run the New Teacher Project, an organization dedicated to getting good teachers into low-income schools, had the enthusiastic support of Joel Klein, the man who holds the chancellor's position in New York City. And Fenty was reaching out to all the school reformers he could find. Before he brought Rhee in, Fenty wrested responsibility from the Board of Education—he, the mayor, would be the person to hold accountable for the success or failure of the city's schools, and the schools would be held accountable for the success or failure of the students. "The only way we're going to become a world-class city," the mayor told Rhee, "is if we fix the public education system."

A lot of fixing is required. And the fact that the whole city is not up in arms over the schools remains a mystery to me—kids in the capital have gotten a truly bum deal. Though Washington spends more money per pupil than almost every other place in the nation, its schools carry the dubious distinction of being rated the worst in the country by various educational organizations. When Mayor Fenty reached out for a radical reformer it was because more than half of the fourth graders scored below basic skill levels in math and almost two-thirds could not achieve a basic reading score. By eighth grade the numbers were reversed but no better. Two-thirds failed at basic math, more than half rated below basic in reading. In an interview with Rhee in a conference room off of the cheery but no-nonsense suite of the chancellor in a D.C. government building near the Capitol, I asked her to describe her reaction to what she found when she showed up for work. "It was sad in lots of ways. If you look at the data, the achievement levels for our kids, it's absolutely phenomenal. We are the only school district in the country that is on high-risk status with the U.S. Department of Education."

One statistic stands out as the "saddest" to Rhee: "Our kindergarteners actually start off relatively equal to kindergarteners in other jurisdictions, and then as time goes on they fall further and further behind so that by the time they're in the third grade, they're well below their counterparts in other cities. And poor black kids in New York City are two grade levels ahead of where our poor black kids are." That shows, says this somewhat fierce young woman, that the poor achievement levels aren't a result of poverty or deprivation: "The social ills in New York are no different than what they are here in D.C. There's no reason why those kids should be two grade levels ahead of our kids." What these kids need, insists Michelle Rhee, is better teachers. She's convinced that it's the teachers that will make the difference—not bringing in the parents, cleaning up the neighborhoods, getting people jobs. Those would all be great ideas, she agrees, but the kids can't wait for all of that: "In our city with the circumstances that so many of our children are in, if we write them off and say until we can get their parents together or until we can fix the problem of poverty then there is nothing that can be done for those kids, then we should just close up shop right now. I think it's the other way around. I think that the problem of poverty will not be solved until we solve the challenges within public education."

Resistance and downright hostility to Rhee's ideas, particularly from some longtime teachers, are enormous. Some of it is understandable. Many dedicated and hardworking teachers have seen Washington serve as something of a guinea pig for experiments in public education. The city has a voucher program, called the Opportunity Scholarship Program, where low-income students can receive federally funded stipends to attend private schools. There's also a robust public charter school movement. Those schools have attracted more and more parents, causing enrollment to drop substantially in the schools under Chancellor Rhee's domain. But still, she lectures, that's no reason to write her schools off: "I strongly believe that choice in public education is incredibly important. And I don't think limiting choice in any way is helpful to the public schools, because at the end of the day what we need is incredibly informed consumers, people who know what they want, who know what a good school looks like."

But, she argues, many parents don't fit the description of the informed consumer: "The parents who are savvy in this city, who have less means, have a lot of options—more options than probably any other city in this country. There are lots of high-performing charter schools, there's the voucher program, the Opportunity Scholarship Program, and so they sort of navigate their way through. Which is great for those kids and those families. But for the kids whose parents are not as engaged, and who are having more of the social problems and that sort of thing, we still are obligated to make sure that those kids have an equal chance in life."

The best way to do that in Michelle Rhee's opinion? There's only one answer—give those kids good teachers. She came to her firm views about the importance of teaching, views that are bolstered by a good deal of research, when, fresh out of Cornell University, she joined Teach for America, the organization that takes elite college graduates and sends them to teach for two years in underserved public schools. When Rhee landed in one of the scariest schools in Baltimore, she experienced what she described as culture shock: "I don't think there's anything like being a first-year teacher in a low-performing, high-poverty urban school," she told me. "I just don't think anything can prepare you for some of the realities. We had no books. We had no supplies. My mother would go to Costco and buy thirty-six pairs of scissors and crayons and send them to us because we just didn't have any. I had a little kid that was so troubled that one day she came into the classroom and her head was sopping wet and I was like, 'What are you doing? What happened?' And she was trying to drown herself in the water fountain because she was so unhappy and her mother was in jail. When you have the background that I do—I grew up very privileged—and you're looking at this little eight-year-old who doesn't want to live, I mean, there aren't a lot of things that can prepare you for that." The childhood of the daughter of a doctor, a Korean immigrant, in Toledo, Ohio, certainly didn't prepare the neophyte teacher who told *Newsweek* magazine about another mouth-dropping day in that school. When the kids were lining up for lunch and one of them fell down, "Each kid, as they were walking by, kicked the kid that was down," she recalled. "I was like, 'What are they doing?' But it was like second nature to them. The kid is down. Kick him." Eventually the shock began to wear off and Rhee got down to the business of learning how to be a good teacher: "I got better as the year went on, and then I spent the summer between my first and second years—all I did was plan, all summer long. I didn't have a job, I didn't do anything. I cut out letters, I photocopied things, I lesson planned, and I knew exactly what I wanted to do when I got back in the classroom the second year. Once that happened and once I had that kind of focus and I knew exactly what goals I had, then it was over."

In that second year, she and a colleague took on the challenge of seventy kids whose test scores were at "almost rock bottom," assigning them homework, convincing their parents to send them to school on Saturdays, and bringing their test scores to be "absolutely at the top" after two years. If she hadn't been convinced before then of the importance of teachers, Michelle Rhee certainly was after that experience: "Those kids, where they lived didn't change. Their parents didn't change. Their diets didn't change. The violence in the community didn't change. The only thing that changed for those seventy kids was the adults who were in front of them every single day teaching them." And then, she told *Time,* "What was most disappointing was to watch these kids go off into the fourth grade and just lose everything" because their teachers "weren't engaging them."

The belief that teachers make all the difference pushed Michelle Rhee to accept the challenge to start the New Teacher Project when the head of Teach for America proposed it to her. After ten years, the program was operating in more than two hundred school districts, with about twenty-eight thousand new teachers. By then Rhee had married a man she met while they were both teaching (they have since separated), graduated from the Kennedy School of Government at Harvard, and had two daughters. Then Fenty convinced her to pack up her kids—their father came along as well—and move to Washington to put her ideas about education reform into practice. So far, despite the unqualified support of the mayor, it hasn't been easy either for the chancellor or the city she's trying to save.

To howls of outrage from parents, teachers, and principals, Rhee closed down twenty-three schools and fired thirty-six principals—a full quarter of the total—plus 270 teachers and more than a hundred bureaucrats from the famously inefficient and bloated central office. She was still somewhat wide-eyed more than a year later as she remembered the response: "The lawyer, the general counsel, came in and he was like, 'You've got to stop firing people.' And I said, 'Why? If they're no good, then we're going to fire them.' And he said, 'Welcome to D.C. public schools, where we never fire anyone.' And then he went through this whole rigmarole of telling me what you had to do to fire someone, and it was literally impossible to do. So I went to the mayor and I said, 'Look, I need to be able to build my own team, and if I have to keep hundreds of people on the payroll that are not just not doing a good job, but are doing a bad job and costing this district money and that sort of thing, this is going to be an impossible task.' And that's when the mayor said, 'Well, you know, if we don't like the rules of the game, we're just going to change the rules.' And that's when we went to get the legislation to make this central office employees at-will employees. And that was the big firestorm, that everybody up until that point said, 'We're supporting you, we want change. Yes, on the revolution.' And then when we dropped that legislation it was like, 'Wait, wait, wait.'"

No word is more calculated to raise Rhee's hackles than

the word *wait,* except perhaps the words *slow down.* To the criticism—and there's a lot of it—that she's moving too fast, doing too much too soon, the chancellor has a ready answer: "You can't go into some of our schools in this city and think that it is possible to move too fast with kids languishing in those environments and in those circumstances." One move that attracted a lot of flak—firing the principal at her own children's school: "My kids were like, 'Why?'" Rhee was amazed that her own daughters echoed the question she had heard from other students when she fired their principals: "'She's not that bad, is she?'" Rhee says with some fire, "And I said, 'That's not the standard that we have. "Not so bad" is not what you deserve.'" Then she adds, in a more subdued tone, "But you know what? It is this sad lowering of expectations that the kids are saying this to me. Right? The children are saying, 'But we've seen worse, and she's not as bad as what we know we could get.' And when the kids have that mind-set and mentality—that just—that kills me."

If the kids sadden Michelle Rhee, some of the adults infuriate her. She tells the story of arguing with a principal over the effectiveness of one teacher. As the principal continued to defend the teacher, the chancellor asked if he would put his own grandchild in that classroom. His answer astonished her: "He said, 'Well, if that's the standard, then I wouldn't put my grandchild in any classroom. We don't have any effective teachers.' And I said, 'That's the standard. Why should we expect anything less for the kids in your school than you do for your grandchild?'" In order to bring in and reward more effective teachers, Rhee came up with a plan that she was sure the teachers would embrace. She convinced private foundations to provide funding for substantial pay increases and then proposed a two-tiered system—red and green—with two different salary schedules. All current teachers would have the right to choose between them. All new teachers would come in under the green plan, which promised enormous increases in salary—salaries public school teachers have never even thought about, with the highest reaching more than $113,000 plus a possible $20,000 bonus tied to student test scores—in exchange for giving up tenure. Those who chose the red plan would also receive hefty salary increases—about 28 percent over five years, but no bonuses—and they would keep their tenure. Rhee believed the plan would meet with surefire success: "When I read the final proposal before we laid it out, I literally thought to myself, 'I am going to be the hero of the Washington, D.C., teachers.' I mean, we are talking about a system that could double their salaries in a profession that everybody says that one of the problems with the profession is that we don't pay people enough. Right? Right now a new teacher in the system makes forty thousand dollars a year. On green, if they are performing at the highest levels, a new teacher could make seventy-eight thousand a year. There aren't very many jobs that you can go into your first year out of college and make eighty thousand dollars. At the higher end, paying up to a hundred and thirty thousand, where those teachers right now make a base salary of sixty-eight thousand. And it was a choice for everyone. That's what I thought was the key. We're not forcing everyone to go on green, you have a choice. If you want to keep your rights and your privileges and whatever, stay on red. And I told George Parker, the union president, I said, 'If everybody wants to stay on red, that's fine. I mean, we just want to give the choice.'" But far from seeing her as a hero, the teacher's union has cast Michelle Rhee as the villain. It's impossible to know where teachers really stand, because the union has never scheduled a vote on the proposed contract, but in a survey of members by a highly reputable polling firm teachers rejected the idea of money in exchange for job security by an almost two-to-one margin. Many of them just don't trust this new brash young woman, and the national teachers' union has gotten involved, accusing Rhee of trying to "break the union" and "kill tenure."

It's certainly true that she has no love for tenure—the system that provides job protection for teachers and professors. "Tenure has no educational value for our children. None. It just doesn't. They can say anything they want, but there is no link between the tenure of a teacher and student achievement levels. And so right now we are all arguing about something that brings no benefit to kids." You can see why the teachers would be nervous. But their refusal to sign a contract hasn't stopped this woman from moving forward with her plans. Without the carrot of bonuses for good teachers, Rhee has decided to use a stick to go after bad teachers—tying their evaluations to student achievement, placing them on probation and firing them if they don't improve. It will be a more contentious, costlier, and more time-consuming way to get the job done, but Michelle Rhee will continue to push out people who don't believe as she does that all children, regardless of their circumstances, can and must get a good education. And she will fight to bring in those who agree with her, knowing that it won't be easy. "It does take a different kind of teacher to be successful with kids who have to face this many challenges, but it can absolutely be done. There's no doubt in my mind."

Her take-no-prisoners attitude and her willingness to tell it like it is have offended some politicians and parents as well as teachers, but her no-beating-around-the-bush style has made her a media darling. She's been the subject of major profiles on radio, on television, and in print. (She, probably unwisely, posed for the cover of *Time* holding a broom.) Every article elicits endless arguments on the blogosphere, with sites representing teachers' unions particularly harsh in their postings. And Rhee's other critics, insisting that they have seen no results from her controversial actions—though test scores have improved—claim that it's the chancellor's love of the spotlight that drives her. But Michelle Rhee does a great deal more than smile for the cameras. She holds regular community forums—where she's often subjected to tirades of abuse (fortunately, she says, she's not a crier)—to talk about school closings and teacher firings; she meets with neighborhood organizations and business groups; she regularly visits all of her schools, and she answers every single e-mail from parents, teachers, and kids herself. Her staff claims it was close to a hundred thousand messages in 2008. She puts in long hours because she knows that she doesn't have much time, that the protectors of the status quo and their political patrons will try to retake the reins of the school system, and that D.C. kids will be the losers. Again. As to her style, she says, "We never got anywhere sitting around singing 'Kumbaya.'" But she also knows how to charm a room.

She's willing to try any approach that works, because the kids deserve it. Why, she asks, shouldn't the children in Washington enjoy the advantages the kids in the nearby sub-urbs take for granted? "We want to prepare them to be able to be productive members of society and to enter the work-place with the sort of skills they need to have a well-paying job so that they can support their families. Just getting a GED is not the answer." The "soft prejudice of low expecta-tions" drives her crazy. And she hears it everywhere, even from city council members who suggest that preparing D.C. kids for college is a waste. If she can help it, Michelle Rhee will not let the politicians give these students short shrift: "Kids who graduate from college make over a million dol-lars more during their lifetime. . . . Whether they choose to go or not, I have to graduate kids who have options in life, that if they want to go to a four-year college, that they are prepared to do so. That's my job." It might not be a job she will be able to do, but she will do everything she humanly can to give the children of the nation's capital a shot at a good education. And remember, it's a job she loves.

ATHLETE

■　　　■　　　■

"GIRLS RULE!" THAT CHEER WENT UP RESOUNDINGLY, WITH accompanying high fives all around the country, as the U.S. women's soccer team won the World Cup in the summer of 1999. Ninety thousand people filled the Rose Bowl and 40 million more watched on television as Brandi Chastain kicked the winning point against China, more people than watched the men's basketball championship.

Then, not quite a decade later, it was an "old" woman who captivated the world when Dara Torres, at age forty-one and with a two-and-a-half-year-old daughter watching, won three silver medals in the 2008 Olympics, missing the gold in one event by one one-hundredth of a second, still breaking the American record. The oldest swimmer ever in the long history of the games, and a veteran of five Olympic competitions, Torres is able to turn her medals into money, with endorsements from Speedo and Toyota and invitations to inspire on the speaking circuit. The women soccer players did the same thing, and several of them are still out on the airwaves, promoting women's sports. It's a very different world from the one Donna de Varona encountered after she swam her way to the gold in the 1960s. De Varona served as the chairman of the Soccer World Cup in 1999 and she's the person who bullied the TV executives into covering it, something that simply would not have happened even a few years earlier. In the aftermath of de Varona's Olympic triumphs, she found no room for her in the wide world of sports—no endorsements, no college scholarships available for a girl gold medalist. That changed when the law changed. In 1972, when Congress passed what's come to be known as Title IX, the law outlawing sex discrimination in education, the lawmakers had no notion that they would be building an enormous arena for women's sports. But that's exactly what happened.

Amazingly, women athletes today are knowledgeable about Title IX and give the law credit almost every time they talk to reporters about the reasons for their success. The people who make money from female sports figures are aware of the law's long reach as well. During the 1996 Olympics, Nike ran commercials showing pictures of the women winners, while a narrator read the actual text of the legislation. And on the triumphal day after the U.S. women's soccer team won the World Cup, Brandi Chastain, with her arms encircling the trophy, sat next to a smiling Donna de Varona on *This Week*. I asked de Varona, who had risked so much convincing the networks to carry the game and then bludgeoning sponsors into going along, whether it could all have happened without Title IX. "No," she answered instantly, "we wouldn't have had those stadiums full. It just wouldn't have happened."

It certainly didn't happen in my childhood. When I was growing up in the 1940s and '50s, the only female athletes I had ever heard of were Gertrude Ederle, the first woman to swim the English Channel, and Babe Didrikson Zaharias, the champion golfer. (I didn't know she had been an Olympic track-and-field star before that.) These were singular women who certainly never appeared sweaty on the Movietone News. And Esther Williams was downright gorgeous, floating around the big screen in flowered bathing caps surrounding her perfectly made-up face. Women playing team sports simply didn't exist, as far as girls my age were concerned. Because I went to a girls' school, I did play on teams, though I was never any good at it. Still, there were female athletic big shots in our midst, which wasn't true at most coeducational schools in the 1950s. And my school's annual Father/Daughter Field Day was a much-anticipated event. I regularly won at leapfrog, but I don't think there's any Olympic category for that; I was also a pretty good sprinter, but it never occurred to me to run the fifty- and hundred-yard dashes any day other than Field Day. (My competitive "sport" was debating, which arguably provided me with more useful training for Sunday mornings with Sam Donaldson and George Will.) When I went to Wellesley, much to my horror, physical education was a requirement. My mother suggested that I try something "useful" like tennis or golf, something I could play when I grew up, as opposed to a team sport. Dutifully, I tried both, only to learn that my hand-eye coordination was so nonexistent that I was asked to play by myself. So much for sports! But every one of us also had to take Fundamentals of Body Movement, or "fundies," for a semester—a sort of combination of calisthenics and etiquette. Actually, though we ridiculed it at the time, learning to get into a car properly has served me in good stead over the years. (Put your rear end on the seat first, then swing your legs around.) We didn't know that the "fundies" requirement was the vestige of a battle that had been going on in women's sports for much of the first half of the twentieth century. Calisthenics was good for young ladies, went the argument of the professional physical education establishment; competition was not.

There's evidence that girls competed in sporting events at least as long ago as the days of ancient Greece, where virgins—no married women were allowed—ran in footraces. A fourth-century Roman mosaic shows girls in skimpy two-piece outfits (thus the name "bikini girls" mosaic), receiving prizes for javelin and discus throwing, long jumping, footracing, and ball playing. Throughout the Middle Ages, fairs would often include women's sporting events, especially footracing and games with bats and balls; and somewhat less savory women boxed and wrestled for ogling onlookers. Some sports were definitely for the upper classes—hunting and riding to hounds, particularly. Mary, Queen of Scots, loved golf. Some sports, such as tennis, attracted the middle class as well. And by the end of the nineteenth century everyone was into cycling. In fact, bicycles became such a source of freedom for women—they could take off on their own without chaperones and replace their long skirts and corsets with free-flowing bloomers—that the great suffragist Elizabeth Cady Stanton said in 1895, "Many a woman is riding to suffrage on a bicycle."

The link between women's equality and women's athleticism was firmly connected both in Great Britain and America as the twentieth century approached. In England a group called the Gymnastic Teachers' Suffrage Society coached girls in all kinds of sports—cricket, lacrosse, field hockey, and tennis. One girls' school adopted the motto Be Your Own Pygmalion. The women's colleges at Oxford and Cambridge competed against each other in all those games. And as women's institutions cropped up in the United States, they fielded teams as well. Two baseball teams played against each other at Vassar in 1866, and in the following years basketball, fencing, rowing, and track were added to the roster. When a young woman broke her leg playing baseball, college president John Howard Raymond insisted she could just as easily have done it on the dance floor, that it was no reason to disband the team. Soon after each of the prestigious women's colleges opened its doors, athletics followed. The students soon found their required calisthenics classes boring, so they militated for competitive sports. Smith College history includes organized basketball in 1893; the Wellesley College annals record a tennis match against Radcliffe in 1897. Before that, on the West Coast, Stanford women battled their sisters at the University of California in a fierce basketball contest in 1896. Men were not allowed to watch the game in the San Francisco Armory Hall because the women would be wearing bloomers (not to mention sweating and very likely exhibiting unladylike behavior), but five hundred women cheered on the basketball players to a Stanford victory.

As women raised their voices calling for equality at the ballot box, the ideal of a healthy, active woman replaced the nineteenth-century fashion of the delicate, weak female. Sports clubs grew up around the country for wealthy women, who were also able to compete in tennis and golf at country clubs and resorts. And the able and athletic Gibson Girl symbolized the "new woman" whom magazine-reading girls tried to copy. In 1900 American Margaret Abbott won the Olympic gold in golf, and European and American women played for championships in archery, golf, and tennis. Writing in *Munsey's Magazine* in 1901, Anne O'Hagen concluded, "With the single exception of the improvement in the legal status of women, their entrance into the realm of sports is the most cheering thing that has happened to them in the century just past."

That was the same year field hockey hit these shores in the person of Constance Applebee. The formidable Englishwoman was a fanatic fan of the sport, which she introduced in an exhibition at Harvard. In 1902 Wellesley hired her to teach the sport there. Then Miss Applebee made the circuit of colleges, spreading the gospel of field hockey, which her disciples were eager to hear. The game, dating back in one form or another to ancient times, caught on quickly, becoming an Olympic sport in 1908, but it must have disappointed Miss Applebee greatly that only the men's game was so honored. As late as the 1950s my sister went to a hockey camp presided over by Miss Applebee, who was still running up and down the field in her brown gymsuit, whistle clenched between her teeth, epithets at the ready. In fact, she continued coaching off and on until the 1970s, when she was in her late nineties. Miraculously, the redoubtable Miss Applebee lived to see women's field hockey become an Olympic sport in 1980—she died the next January, a month shy of her 108th birthday.

Though the twentieth century looked like a welcoming era for women athletes when it began, as in so many other areas of women's lives, sports followed no straight-line progression. Magazines and newspapers warned that women were endangering their childbearing capabilities with so much activity, making themselves unattractive by developing their muscles, and sacrificing their femininity to the playing field. (Historians assert that unspoken fears of lesbianism underlay much of the concern about women and athletics.) With the success of the suffrage movement in 1920, many women's organizations lost their sense of purpose, and the twenties and thirties saw female colleges moving away from any kind of competition. Some team sports at women's colleges simply disappeared. The women's division of the Amateur Athletic Union advised against intercollegiate matches for women, arguing that they benefited the few star athletes over the many students who might want to play, and that men's intercollegiate sports had been wracked by scandal. The physical education establishment also thought it was immodest to have men watch women play, so they promoted intramural games that they thought the guys wouldn't be interested in. Play days were encouraged. At these daylong events women from different schools would join together on teams, so no school rivalries could form. When the Olympic Games added women's track and field in 1928, the American Women's Division of the AAU asked the organizers of the games not to repeat the event.

The sports establishment effectively spread its message. In 1924 women at 22 percent of a sampling of American colleges participated in intercollegiate sports, but by 1931 the number had dropped to 12 percent. And although 60 percent of the respondents in 1924 said that women could be physically harmed by intercollegiate competition, seven years later almost 80 percent held that view. The proscription against women's competition continued as official policy well into the 1950s. In 1957, three years before I entered college, the organization for amateur athletes was still calling for women's play days rather than intercollegiate competition. (The idea that women were too delicate for competition spread to other endeavors as well. When I was at Wellesley, three women ran against one another for all student government offices, instead of the usual two, with a wildly complicated proportional voting system, so there wouldn't be one winner and one loser.)

But most women didn't go to college, and many members of the less pampered set were happily competing in sports, unaware of the "damage" they might be causing themselves. At the beginning of the twentieth century, just about every town had a baseball team. Men and women all over the country were baseball crazed, so showmen and impresarios tried to capitalize on the fever by coming up with gimmicks for female teams. The Springfield (Illinois) Blondes and Brunettes played only four games in 1875, but the idea of fielding a team of all blondes against one of all brunettes was too good to die. In 1883 it was the Philadelphia Blondes and Brunettes. Also that year the all-female Philadelphia Red Stockings played their sister team, the Blue Stockings, and to boost attendance, women were admitted free. When five hundred women showed up at the Camden, New Jersey ball field, the management decided to charge them admission— the children's price of fifteen cents. Most successful were the Bloomer Girls teams, which barnstormed around the country, playing men's town teams and minor-league teams from Texas to Nova Scotia in the period from the 1890s to the 1920s. The Bloomer Girls were particularly popular during World War I, when they traveled as far as Cuba and Japan to show off their sport. With the help of a couple of male ringers (called "toppers" because of the wigs they wore to look like women), these indefatigable players toured tirelessly. In 1903 the Boston Bloomers played and won twenty-eight games in twenty-six days; on July 3 and 4, they pitched and hit through six games in five different Oklahoma towns.

If something of a Harlem Globetrotters–like show was performed by the Bloomer Girls, some other female baseball players were deadly serious. Alta Weiss started pitching for the Vermilion (Ohio) Independents in 1907, becoming such a phenomenon on the male semiprofessional team that she was able to put herself through college and medical school from her earnings. Special trains ran from Cleveland to Vermilion when the "Girl Wonder" pitched. On a couple of occasions Weiss faced another female pitcher for a men's team on the diamond, and even after she started practicing medicine she kept pitching. But the "Queen of Baseball," according to New England fans, was Lizzie Murphy. The first baseman (basewoman?) joined the Providence Independents, a semiprofessional team, in 1918 and then signed up with the All-Stars of Boston, where she played exhibition games against major-league teams until her retirement in 1935. Jackie Mitchell's moment in the sun in 1931 is a bit more controversial. As a publicity stunt, the manager of the Chattanooga Lookouts, a minor-league team, recruited the seventeen-year-old pitcher and sent her to the mound in an exhibition game against the New York Yankees. The teenager managed to strike out the mighty Babe Ruth and Lou Gehrig in back-to-back at bats. You can still get an argument going about whether the Yankee legends were just putting on a show, but Mitchell's insistence that she struck them out fair and square has been backed up by some Yankee players. Soon after the game the baseball commissioner, Kenesaw Mountain Landis, voided Mitchell's contract with the Chattanooga team, saying baseball was too strenuous for a woman. When another team tried to sign a woman in 1952, organized baseball officially banned women from the minor leagues; this ban has never been lifted.

In 1992 the movie *A League of Their Own* finally told America the story of the All-American Girls Professional Baseball League, which entertained on the home front during World War II. The brainchild of Chicago Cubs owner Philip Wrigley, the league recruited skilled female players from softball diamonds and industrial teams, with the intention of having them play serious baseball. Wrigley also insisted that the women be well mannered and groomed, with charm and etiquette classes provided by Helena Rubinstein. No smoking, drinking, or unauthorized dating was allowed on the highly chaperoned road trips, and lipstick was included in the regulation uniform, which also featured short skirts and long hair. The rule book for the league instructed the women on what to pack by way of clothes (dark suits and easily laundered blouses) and toiletries (cleansing cream, medium rouge) and how to act in all situations: "In a final summing up, be neat and presentable in your appearance and dress, be clean and wholesome in appearance, be polite and considerate in your daily contacts, avoid noisy, rough and raucous talk and actions and be in all respects a truly All American girl." Despite the feminine trappings, these women could play. With team names like the Racine Belles, the Fort Wayne Daisies, the Grand Rapids Chicks, and the Springfield Sallies, the women attracted close to a million fans at the height of their popularity in 1948. More than six hundred women played professional baseball, becoming heroines to thousands of little girls. But with the end of the war and the resulting pressure on women to leave the workplace, the league eventually died. It was all but forgotten until the 1980s, when the Baseball Hall of Fame was persuaded to honor these women among its exhibits.

While college women were subjected to debates over what was proper in competition, working-class women had no highbrow theories holding them back. They found lots of opportunities to participate in various sports as an extension of their work. Businesses formed teams as morale boosters, but the bosses were dead serious about winning, so they would recruit good athletes and then find jobs for them. It was this industrial league that brought to world attention the woman some consider the best all-around athlete of all time—Babe Didrikson Zaharias—who reigned unchallenged as the greatest female athlete in the twentieth century until Jackie Joyner-Kersee came along. Babe Didrikson was playing basketball for her high school in Beaumont, Texas, in 1930 when the Employers Casualty Company of Dallas came calling—offering a place on the company team and throwing in a job as well. The young woman quickly won basketball honors from the Amateur Athletic Union and then added track records to her accomplishments. In the qualifying competition for the 1932 Olympics, she broke world records in the javelin, eighty-meter hurdles, high jump, and baseball throw. Though she qualified for five sports, women were allowed to compete in only three of them—and she captured the gold in two, the silver in one. She then took her show on the road—first with her own basketball team, then playing with a baseball team—and it was quite a show. Didrikson drew the public and delighted the press, for the most part. There was some sniping at her lack of femininity, including such snide comments as sportswriter Paul Gallico's judgment that Babe "couldn't compete with women in their own and best game—man-snatching." She could certainly compete with men—pitching spring training for major-league teams and taking the mound in exhibition games, while tossing off seventeen sets of tennis or creaming her opponents in bowling. When Didrikson took up golf, she softened her "Texas Tomboy" image and acquired wrestler George Zaharias as a husband. But her determination to win stayed just as solid as ever. In 1946 she won thirteen golf tournaments in a row; the next year she turned pro and a few years later helped found the Ladies Professional Golf Association. Year after year the Associated Press voted her best woman athlete of the year, even after a bout with cancer caused her to play a season with a colostomy. That cancer soon killed her, only in her midforties, with her phenomenal career still soaring.

Tuskegee University, the famous black college, also trained women athletes at a time when predominately white schools did not. Track-and-field stars there went on to train other black women—most notably the female phenomenon of the 1960 Olympics, Wilma Rudolph. The twentieth of twenty-two children born to a railroad porter father and a cleaning woman mother, Rudolph had several crippling diseases as a little girl growing up in Clarksville, Tennessee. A bout with polio put her leg in a brace for several years, but remarkably, after she shed the brace, the young girl took up basketball and then track, traveling as the youngest member of the team to the 1956 Melbourne Olympics. Then, in her senior year of high school, Rudolph gave birth to an illegitimate baby. Her parents refused to allow her to marry, insisting that she continue her education. Wilma went to Tennessee State University; the baby went to live with Wilma's grandmother. In 1960 in Rome, in the first Olympic Games widely seen on American television, she became the first woman to win three track-and-field gold medals in a single Olympics, making her an inspiration for female athletes following in her fleet footsteps like the great Jackie Joyner-Kersee. After her record-setting triumph, Rudolph competed for one more season; she then married her baby's father and set up a foundation for underprivileged children.

Wilma Rudolph's triumphs burst into the national consciousness just as women were beginning to demand equality in all aspects of life. The modern women's movement of the 1960s and '70s found its stalwarts on the tennis courts as well as in courts of law. Foremost among them was then—and remains today—Billie Jean King, who was ranked the number one woman tennis player in the world five times. She's battled relentlessly against the discrepancy in prize money awarded to male and female tennis champions, successfully organizing a boycott of the sponsors of the Pacific Southwest Championship. In that event, the male winner took home $12,500 along with his trophy; the female, $1,500. Finally, after an almost twenty-year war, in 2007 King knocked over the last holdout when Wimbledon agreed to equal prize money. The fight was not about the money, she insisted to me: "It's about the message. It's empowering girls to think they can do anything." I interviewed King in 2008 for *USA Weekend* magazine as the Sports Museum of America was set to open in New York. Included in the museum is the Billie Jean King International Women's Sports Center, the first permanent hall of fame and women's sports exhibit in America. "I don't want girls, or boys, to ever think they're inferior. Everyone deserves the dream."

Billie Jean King knew that the dream for girls could be in jeopardy if she lost what ranks as by far her most famous match—against Proud-to-Be-a-Male-Chauvinist Bobby Riggs. "I was a mess because I knew what it meant," she remembered all too well thirty-five years later. "It was about social change. Remember, Title IX had just been passed, and I did not want us to go backwards." Thirty thousand spectators showed up in Houston's Astrodome, with another 40 million tuning in on TV, to watch what was indeed a spectacle. Despite the ridiculous trappings (she came in on a feathered litter carried by musclemen; he rode a golden-wheeled rickshaw pulled by girls called Bobby's Bosom Buddies), the women of the world cheered King on as she beat the pants off Riggs in three straight sets. That was in 1973—the same year King founded the Women's Tennis Association and three years after she had organized the Virginia Slims professional tennis tour. The next year she formed the Women's Sports Foundation, with Donna de Varona as its first president and chair, to promote athletic opportunities for girls and women. The foundation advocates for girls in sports, conducts and propagates research, and provides programs like GoGirlGo! aimed at getting girls active. (Many years later, she also founded the Billie Jean King Foundation to help support gay and lesbian youth, among others. King had been "outed" when she was sued for support by a woman who was an ex-lover, which made it hard for her to cash in with postretirement product endorsements.)

When King and de Varona started organizing on behalf of women athletes, they knew they had a powerful new teammate in Title IX. In 1972, when Congress passed a new education law, it included language—in the ninth section, or title, of the bill—outlawing gender discrimination in any educational institution that received federal funds. The language is simple: "No person in the United States shall, on the basis of sex, be excluded from participation in, be denied the benefits of, or be subjected to discrimination under any educational program or activity receiving federal financial assistance." The antidiscrimination language applied schoolwide, in all disciplines, including athletics. Since federal money flows into almost every school in one way or another, a revolution occurred almost overnight—vastly increasing girls' athletic participation, by 904 percent in high school and 456 percent in college! And girls started getting athletic scholarships to go to college—something almost unheard-of before the law was passed. The before and after Title IX numbers in athletic programs are downright shocking. Take the University of Washington as an example: In

1973–74, men's sports were allotted $2.5 million; women's sports, eighteen thousand dollars. By the next year, the women's allotment was up to two hundred thousand dollars. Overall National Collegiate Athletic Association budgets for women in the largest and most competitive Division 1 schools went from 2 percent to 14 percent in four years. Women's intercollegiate competitions became big draws on campus. So much for the Amateur Athletic Union of old.

As with all revolutions, this one has had its share of resistance from the good old boys trying to hold on to power, sometimes going to absurd lengths to avoid complying with the law. When a court ruled that Brown University violated Title IX by refusing to reinstate its women's gymnastics and volleyball programs, the school spent more than a million dollars in legal fees in a failed appeal to the Supreme Court rather than coughing up the sixty-six thousand dollars for the programs. Every few years, big football colleges persuade their friends in Congress to try to weaken the law, and promoters of women's athletics believe some loopholes have wormed their way into the basic fabric of equality. The Supreme Court posed the biggest threat in its *Grove City* decision, which ruled that only the departments that received federal funds would be affected by antidiscrimination laws, not the entire school. With few athletic programs drawing money directly from Washington, women's sports were in jeopardy until Congress passed a law restating its intention that *all* programs in a school would be covered by the antidiscrimination statute. President Ronald Reagan's veto of what was called the Civil Rights Restoration Act was soundly overridden.

Still, activists for women in sports point to the inequities faced by any little girl who thinks her shot at making it on the playing field is equal to her brother's. Men's sports still get the bulk of the budget, male athletes still get the lion's share of the scholarships, female coaches are few and far between, and their head-coach numbers are growing smaller, not larger, as women's teams are taken more seriously. It will continue to require the vigilance of advocates in the courts and on the campuses to enforce the law. But now they have so many people rooting for them—the mothers and fathers of the little girls out every Saturday on the soc-cer fields of the suburbs, the fanatic fans of the women's basketball teams who've turned out in record numbers, and all those glorious Olympic gold medal winners—fifty-seven of them in 2008, many in team sports.

Women have enjoyed success in the wider world of sports as well. In 2008 even rough-and-tumble ice hockey in-ducted a woman—Cammi Granato—into its Hall of Fame. Granato led the U.S. women's ice hockey team to a gold medal in the 1998 Olympics in Japan, the first time women's ice hockey was included in the games, and then she went on to a career as a radio commentator with the Los Angeles Kings. When the Women's National Basketball Association started in 1996, it garnered lucrative TV contracts while magazines featured stories about player Sheryl Swoopes as demon scorer and devoted mother. And basketball viewership has continued to climb—the championship game in 2008 saw a 30 percent increase over 2007, compared with an 8 percent drop for the men's final. And now women own some of those teams, have their hands on the real power. But, even with all of the enormous change over the last thirty-five years, Billie Jean King reminds us that there's still a long way to go: "We're shockingly off. Just for example, we get eight percent of the sports page—horses and dogs get about seven percent, or about what we do. We have one billion dollars in sponsorship worldwide—men have over twenty-five billion. And that's just the beginning. We have so far to go in the sports world."

King lives and breathes the numbers every day. She knows how much smaller the salaries of female athletes and coaches are than those of their male colleagues; she knows that though the average purse in women's golf has risen to more than a million dollars, for men it's over five million; she knows how underrepresented women are on the committees that run sports matches. So it's understandable that she sees the half-empty glass. But as someone looking in from outside, I'm on the half-full side. I know women's schools—both colleges and secondary schools—have learned that they have to build up-to-date athletic facilities to attract top students. I've talked to little-girl aspiring athletes who see a completely different sports universe from the one their mothers encountered. The girls can look at pictures of women's teams on their Wheaties boxes at breakfast; pick up the newspaper and get the scores of women's events on the sports pages; and on TV see ads featuring female players, watch a women's college game, and hear female sports reporters providing the play-by-play for professional games. None of that was true a generation ago when Donna de Varona was just about the only big-time female sportscaster. When I put it that way to Billie Jean King, she didn't hesitate: "I know, but that's not how I'm made. You're absolutely correct. If I pause and embrace it, it's great that we got this far. But what's that got to do with today and tomorrow?"

Today and tomorrow Billie Jean King will be out there fighting for all the future female athletes—the gold medal girls coming along and their ability to turn pro: "They need to see professional opportunities—so they can stay in what they love, what they're highly skilled in, and make a living." It is, after all, what all of us want to do.

FRIEND

■　　　■　　　■

WHAT WOULD WE DO WITHOUT OUR WOMEN FRIENDS? I
can't imagine how we could survive without the hugs and
humor, the closeness and Kleenex that our female friendships provide. Men often envy the importance that friends
play in our lives—and they should. It's a special relationship
women share that most men seem to have trouble achieving. For all the talk about male bonding, I think a lot of
men find friendship with a woman easier than friendship
with another man. I know my husband does. Obviously,
I'm no expert here and volumes have been written by those
who are; all I can talk about with any authority is my own
personal experience.

From the time my father went to Congress, when Barbara

and Tommy were babies and I wasn't yet born, our family lived in Washington while Congress was in session, which was from January into the summer, and in New Orleans when it was on recess, from summertime till January. When Barbara started school, our bi-city existence meant switching in the middle of a grade from one school to another, and that's what we did for many years. We always joked that by the time the teachers caught on to us we were out of there. But our parents caught on and determined we would be better educated if we stayed put. So, in the fall of 1952, when I was eight, we started going to school year-round in Washington. Because I left school in New Orleans as such a little kid, I didn't have many friends there, unlike my sister and brother. When I arrived "home," as we called it, for the summer, the other kids were already separated into their little cliques where there wasn't any room for me, and I missed my Washington friends terribly. We would write long letters saying absolutely nothing, pore over them, and eagerly await the next. My cousins, who had no choice in the matter, became my best friends in Louisiana. In the end that's been a boon for me because family ties keep us close, closer than I would be with other childhood friends. And after my sister died it was especially important to me to have the comfort of family members who had shared my childhood.

One cousin, Jo Pepper Tuepker, is related to me on both my mother's and father's sides. (Don't ask.) When we were little kids I would haughtily tell her that she had no relatives who weren't also my relatives, but I had relatives who weren't also hers. Since she is one of seven children, it didn't break her heart to lose out on the extended relative lottery. Jo's mother is my father's sister, and I spent long periods of the summer in the family compound on the Mississippi Gulf Coast where she and my grandparents and other aunts and uncles all lived. After we got tired of the scene there, Jo Pepper and I would board a Trailways bus and travel to Pointe Coupee Parish in Louisiana where my mother's mother, who was also Jo's aunt, would take over. We whiled away part of the long sultry summer on horseback, riding into the tiny town of Lettsworth where there was a general store and a post office and exploring the various haunts on the farm. (It belonged to my grandmother's second husband's brother-in-law, no kin to us whatsoever, but "Uncle Billy" put up with us year in and year out.) Mostly we read. One summer I read all of *Gone with the Wind* out loud to Jo and quizzed her at the end of each chapter to make sure she was listening. As the youngest child in my family, I was thrilled to have someone younger than me to boss around, even though the difference in our ages is only six months. We still laugh a lot about that summer and others where we wondered what all those words meant in the *Reader's Digest* condensed version of *The Grapes of Wrath* and other such steamy (for the 1950s) novels.

My cousins Courtney and Barbara Manard were just on either side of me in age, and lived only six blocks away in

New Orleans. We took swimming lessons together at the local park and somehow survived without contracting some dread disease, then we went back to their house where we devised and acted out myriad imaginary tableaux. I'd tag along with them to their grandmother's house, even though she was no relation to me, where we all played a mean game of canasta. Their other grandmother, my great-aunt, lived near Baton Rouge on a Spanish-moss-draped tree-studded plantation. There picking pecans consumed our time—after all, we were paid eleven cents a pound. Barbara and Courtney now live near me in suburban Washington, and every so often we look at one another and wonder how this happened. How did we three little girls who played endless hours of fantasy games together end up as grandmothers and great-aunts? Where, we ask the clichéd question, did those years go?

It's especially easy for me to lose track of the passing years because I live in the house I grew up in. We moved here when I was eight years old, the year my parents decided we should spend the school year here. It's odd in modern America to settle into the family homestead; it's particularly odd in the Washington, D.C., area, where almost everyone hails from someplace else. People often ask me what it's like to cook in my mother's kitchen, to sleep in my parents' bedroom. Actually, it's quite wonderful. In the years after Steve and I were married and moved away, we took a part of home with us. My parents' early-nineteenth-century cherry bed had been moved to the attic when they went for a king-size model. Steve and I decided to liberate it, and Mamma drove it in a U-Haul to New York (that was something to behold!) where we installed it in our first apartment. The bed then moved around the world with us to California and Greece, until it came back to the old bedroom in Bethesda. There it remains.

Living in my mother and father's house has allowed for continuity for the family over the decades, plus continuing friendships. My sister and I went to Stone Ridge, a private Catholic girls' school run by the rigorously intellectual but also deeply fun-loving Religious of the Sacred Heart. The nuns took us seriously as young women, making it clear that we could be anything we wanted to be in this society. (I tease them now that the only role they tacitly closed off to us was that of priest, and they clearly weren't happy about that.) We were part of the group of kids who ran the student government, acted in the plays, organized the events, put out the school newspaper and yearbook. I was the klutzy one, but the others all starred on the athletic teams, which even in that era counted at a girls' school. The daring stuff we did was so square as to be embarrassing—sneaking cigarettes, driving by boyfriends' houses to see if they were home, listening to Johnny Mathis and the Kingston Trio in one another's dens when we should have been studying. Little did we know then that the friendships formed from those silly pastimes, the countless hours on the telephone, the sleepovers where no one slept, would in later years bring us back together through happy times and sad—through marriages and births and deaths, runaway kids and runaway husbands.

Barbara and I were one of three groups of sisters in our respective grades. Until she died my sister stayed close with my friends' older sisters, and they are still part of our family lives. Clare Pratt became the first American woman to rise to Superior General of the Religious of the Sacred Heart, the order of nuns that taught us. She lived in Rome for many years, and when my mother was there as U.S. ambassador to the Vatican, Clare would keep an occasional eye on her, no easy task. And I kept in touch with her mother here. Clare's sister Cinda was not only my best friend in high school, we roomed together in college as well. She lives in the San Francisco Bay Area, so when my daughter lived there, they would see each other. Becca and her brood regularly went to seders at Cinda's house. My sister's classmate Carol Sweeterman had so much history with our family that she didn't shy away from telling Steve years ago that he wasn't doing the right thing by our son, Lee, who desperately wanted to switch from public to private school. Steven objected for reasons that had little to do with Lee's own needs, and Carol had the standing to tell Steve the hurtful truth. Then Carol and I found ourselves sharing breast cancer stories. Her sister, Anne, my old and good friend, comes to town often to see her daughter Laura, who happens to be my son's friend.

Blessedly, our house seems to attract the children of our old friends, returning like homing pigeons to the place their mothers spent so much of their young lives.

Going to a women's college meant making even more solid friendships that we've easily nurtured over time. Several times in recent years, a group of us have even managed to escape to what my son only slightly jokingly calls "sisterhood is powerful" getaways. After the few years at Wellesley where we all lived under the same roof, we spread out over the country, so we have to make a concerted effort to see one another. Since several of our kids are each other's godchildren, we often use them as an excuse, and whenever we reunite we're only sorry that we don't do it more often; it's remarkable how we're able to pick up the conversation where we left off, even though on the face of it we lead wildly different lives.

It's interesting how in each stage of life new female friends emerge, and how they stay friends forever. Since I first wrote this book, its editor Claire Wachtel and I have worked together on three more where we've continued to crack each other up. And each of my very clever children has managed to marry someone with a great mother! What a pleasure to share grandmothering with Judy McDonald and Flicky Hartman, feisty and fun coconspirators. It's truly special to form such close bonds at this stage of life.

As a young working girl fresh out of college, my friend Eden Lipson, whom I had met through student politics, thankfully came to Washington, which seemed like a real "guy place" at the time. (Maybe it still does, but I'm so used to it, how would I know?) One of the last of my friends to get married—remember, this was the midsixties when you were deemed an old maid at twenty-two—Eden could be counted on to visit us wherever we moved, and to introduce us to her legions of friends while there. Once in California with my second child about due we were driving across a winding canyon road when I started having contractions. Eden managed to keep me, not yet two-year-old Lee, and the car under control until things calmed down. Rebecca didn't arrive for a few more days, but that experience cemented the friendship across the generations even before birth, and when Eden had children later, and named one as my godson, we fortunately also became close. As I write this, it's been more than two years since my dear friend was diagnosed with pancreatic cancer, and just about two years since the doctors told us not to expect her to live through one particularly terrifying night. In that time, as Eden herself has shown incredible toughness and humor, her daughter Margo has been her mother's rock and her shield. Margo and I have spent many a day in the hospital, many a night on the phone. We've tried to counsel and comfort each other across our age span of almost forty years.

Differences in age can be wonderfully useful in these female friendships. While I was working in Washington after college, my boss asked if my mother might know someone who could work for just a few days a week, maybe a young mother. Mamma instantly came up with the name Jean Firstenberg because she had helped with the Johnson inauguration. Even though she's only eight years older than I am, Jeannie became the older woman I could confide in, the way I now am for younger women at work. We'd go to her house after work to sip Dubonnet and strategize schemes to convince Steve to propose while her kids, Debbie and Doug, then seven and five, vied with me for their mom's attention. For a while, as grown-ups, Debbie worked with my son, Lee, in London, and Doug and his wife, Suzanne, are my neighbors and good friends in Washington, their daughter Lindy, named for my mother, is Steve's and my godchild.

Back those many years ago, it was hard on me when my confidante Jeannie moved to New York, but I soon followed after Steven and I got married. (He finally did propose by saying, "Oh, okay, Cokie.") I was especially glad to have her as a buddy because most of our friendships were pretty well determined by the *New York Times,* where Steve was a (very) young reporter. We hung out with other *Times-*men (and they were men) and their wives, and all the talk was of the *Times.* The overheated institutional gossip served as the common currency for the men, most of whom have not stayed in close touch. For the women, though we participated in the conversation and enjoyed the juicy tidbits at least as much as the guys, it turned out something deeper and much longer lasting was also being said—"I am your friend, I understand you, you can count on me." More than forty years later most of the men are no longer at the *Times* and several of the couples are no longer together, but the women still matter a great deal to one another. When Rebecca got married, some of those old friends gave her a shower. When it came time to write this book, I turned for help with the research to one of them, Ann Charnley, who had been a guest at my very first dinner party. Annie has worked with me on all the books that came after this one as well. Who knew when we pulled this small volume together that we were embarking on a cottage industry?

Intensity, I think, characterizes the friendships you make when your children are small. The hours spent together huddled in chilly playgrounds, held hostage in fast-food restaurants, or holding one another's tear-streaked toddlers creates an intimacy that isn't always there in later life. In my case in those years, particularly strong friendships were forged by tragedy. We had moved to California and made some casual acquaintances, and an old friend from school worked with me on a TV show, but there wasn't that instant circle of colleagues that the *Times* provided in New York. Steve was one of only a few people in the Los Angeles Bureau and he was on the road much of the time. Then some Washington friends asked friends of theirs in California to look us up and they kindly did. At their house I met Millie Harmon, and we hit it off instantly, so Lee, who was just one year old, and I joined her in a weekly playgroup with another friend of hers. In 1970, while Steve and I were visiting our parents over the summer, Millie's twenty-nine-year-old husband was killed in a rafting accident. She had three little children, no sisters and brothers; her husband had no sisters or brothers; his parents were dead; and her father was dead. It was clear that her friends would be her family. And so we were.

We spent many waking hours together. We granted her crying rights for herself, and bragging rights for her children. We spent all significant days and holidays as a newly crafted family. When not quite a year had passed since Ellis had been killed, Millie said, "I'd like to do one of these holidays myself, I think I'm ready." She decided that an Easter brunch would work for her, and I was relieved, since I was cooking the annual Passover seder and it was going to be a lot of entertaining in just a few days' time. So we agreed on a plan. Millie said, "Then it's set, you do Passover, I'll do Easter." Then we burst out laughing—she's Jewish, you see, and I'm Catholic. But that's the way it was for many years and still Millie almost always makes it to Passover at our house.

When a few years later the airplane my father was traveling in disappeared, it was Millie's turn to console me. While I was in Alaska for the early days of the search, Lee turned four. We had a birthday party scheduled at Disneyland the next weekend. Millie got the cake and organized the kids so that when I returned all I had to do was try to cope with

Winnie the Pooh for President while reeling from the still unsolved mystery of my father's disappearance.

During the time we were in Greece, Millie met a terrific guy and they eventually got married. It was a treat when they settled in New York after we had moved back to Washington—no longer did a continent divide us. The other close couple from those terrible but tender days in California, Meredith and Tom Brokaw, had also migrated to New York, so happy days were here again. Then, shockingly, incredibly, Millie's second husband was killed in a car crash. And the circle of friends closed around her again. It seemed only a few years before that I had spoken at their wedding; now I was speaking at his funeral.

As exciting and interesting as it was, going to Greece to live meant leaving thirty years of friends behind. Fortunately, our kids were three and five, so my first task was finding schools for them. With school comes community, and with community comes friendship. I've often said that I would never move again without school-age children— they force you out of any innate shyness. A couple of my good friends from the time in Greece now live in the United States and we've kept in touch over the years, visiting one another in good times, reaching out to one another in bad. Eli and Townsend Friedman, another Jewish/Catholic couple, and their girls, Patricia and Elisa, became especially close. We spent feast days of all flavors together both in Athens and at home. One night when Eli and Patricia returned from apartment-hunting in New York, Townsend was not there to meet them at the train station, as he had promised. Several horrible hours later, they learned the tragic news: he had had a heart attack and fallen into the C&O Canal. Over the next few years, each of the girls got married, and, in the absence of their father, each called on Steve to perform some duty at their weddings. (He actually presided as the "rabbi" at Patricia's. Long story.) And Patricia has turned to me as an experienced older woman as she seeks the ever elusive balance of work and motherhood. Sometimes it seems impossible that the attractive, accomplished woman I am counseling was once that little girl on the beach in Greece.

While we were abroad lots of friends came to visit, and friends would hand their friends who were traveling to the Aegean our phone number. Eden told her buddies Aaron Latham and Lesley Stahl to give us a call. We had never met them but were delighted to invite them over. Lesley still talks about that day, watching me carry Becca, who was so big her body practically covered mine, and seeing what a kick we got from our kids. She and Aaron decided on the spot that a child was a good idea, and proceeded to produce one. I've always teased Taylor Latham that she should be grateful that Lee and Becca were behaving well that day. I knew instantly that Lesley and I would be fast friends if we ever ended up in the same city at the same time.

That opportunity came when we moved back to Washington and I learned the unmatchable value of female friends in the workplace. I was pretty depressed about the move. That's an understatement—I was a first-class witch about it. I felt that I had just gotten my sea legs as a reporter, successfully freelancing for CBS News and several magazines, that my kids were a good age to stay abroad, and that Steve's folks and my mother were still young and healthy enough that they didn't need us back in the United States. I really wanted to see more of the world through another foreign posting, but I was counting on Steve to do that for me—I had no offers of my own, and as far as I was concerned at the time, no opportunities of my own. But the *New York Times* had other plans, and Steven was ready to return to Washington, so I had no choice but to come along, kicking and screaming the whole way. (Well, I could have come along nicely, but what fun would that have been?) We waited to move until the school year was about to begin, so the kids wouldn't be hanging around all summer bored and friendless. Then we barged in on Mamma, who moved into my old room with Rebecca and gave Steven and me the master bedroom. There was a flurry of shopping for school clothes for the kids and work clothes for Steve, as it had been a while since he had been on a beat where a suit was required. Then the day came when I waved them all off in their new outfits to their new lives and went back inside my old home and burst into tears. What now for me? The prospect of pounding the pavement for a job—something I had done over and over as we moved around the country and the world—that prospect was so disheartening I could hardly stand it. Although I had already had a couple of preliminary interviews, I knew it wasn't going to be easy.

When Steven got to work he found himself seated next to a woman he didn't know. She told him that she had just been hired and had been working at National Public Radio. "Does that mean your job there's now open?" my always-on-the-alert husband asked. "Yes," she answered, "why?" "Because I have a wife looking for a job." "Call Nina Totenberg" came the response. He called and Nina said, "Get her résumé right over here." He did, and the rest, as they say, is history. In any event, that's the way Steven tells the story.

The rest, actually, was a good bit harder than that. But it was made considerably easier, as my life has been made easier in the more than thirty years since, by the fact that Nina Totenberg and Linda Wertheimer were at NPR, urging me on, and egging on the bosses to hire me. Linda had graduated from Wellesley the year after I did, and though we didn't know each other there, the alma mater tie existed. It was the first time in my more than a dozen years in the workforce that anything resembling an old girls' network existed. Nina and Linda helped me learn the things I didn't know, forced the guys to acknowledge the things I did know, and supported me through the treacherous first few months when the bosses couldn't decide whether to hire me or not, even though they were putting my stories on the air every day. Finally the three of us succeeded in getting me the job—believe me, it would not have happened had I just been on my own.

We were in our early thirties then; in the years since, we have had the kind of working relationship and familial relationship that's rare at best, impossible more often. On the job, we've filled in for one another by showing up someplace where the other ones can't be, filling in facts in a story, doing some extra reporting that gives it extra heft, or listening to something sensitive to make sure we're not courting trouble. We've also helped fight one another's battles so consistently that a boss knows he's likely to be taking on all three of us if he gets crossways with one of us. For years we sat together in the newsroom, where both our high-volume laughter and our low-pitched whispers seemed to intimidate the men, much to our delight. One horrified colleague called our little corner "the Fallopian Jungle." (But we're still there and he's not!) In truth what we were doing was sharing—sharing joys, hopes, fears, and sorrows. We had at last in the world of work found women like ourselves. We had suffered discrimination and harassment at a time when that just simply was the way it was and now we were in positions of some influence in our organization where we could help one another and the younger women coming along after us.

But our friendship far transcends the shared stories of the workplace. Lots has happened to us in these thirty-plus years. Soon after I went to NPR, Nina got married, and Linda and

I were her ushers. Linda lost her mother and I lost my sister and we kept one another together through those times. When Barbara was sick, Linda and Nina spelled each other on vacation so that I wouldn't be alone. When she died, Linda and her husband, Fred, came rushing home from vacation to be with me. My friends held me, shaking and sobbing, knowing the depths of what I felt, and knowing they would have to get me through the next few painful months.

Right before her fiftieth birthday, Nina's husband took a fall on the ice that caused his brain to hemorrhage. He spent months in intensive care, then in a regular hospital room, then in rehabilitation. Linda and I were there with Nina, sitting through lectures from the neurosurgeon, using our reporting skills first to understand the workings of the brain, and then the workings of the health care system. Floyd finally went home and was well on his way to mending when a routine checkup showed a spot on his lungs. There followed another several months of near-fatal experiences after lung surgery. Nina and Floyd were both incredibly valiant through all of this, but Nina would be the first to say that she could not have done it without her friends keeping vigil with her. When Floyd died the circle widened to embrace other women who cared deeply about Nina, but then, after a while, as it always does, it shrank again. The many mourners gave way to the familiar few.

Then, oh so happily, our friend Nina fell in love. And the wonderful David, whose wife had also died, moved to

Washington to be with his love. Linda and I joined Nina's blood-sisters in holding the chuppah at her wedding. (The wedding canopy was our creation, and we got more than a little grief about it sagging in the middle.)

Though we three have a particularly close relationship, the support system of women working in Washington is wonderfully strong. For years we had a fabulously frivolous ladies' lunch where we traded tales of the people in our trades, and tips on the problems of being our age. Hot gossip and hot flashes shared equal billing. But there were times when other purposes took precedence. At one lunch a member of our group walked in looking stricken. She had just been fired that morning. Lesley Stahl got right on the phone, and by the end of the day, our friend had a job. It was a moment we'll always remember because it showed that finally we could do what the guys had always been able to do—that we had the power to come through for our friends beyond offering a shoulder to cry on. These ritual meals women take together provide food for the soul. The women in the Senate hold regular dinner meetings, which make their male colleagues hilariously nervous but give the women a brief respite from the pomposity and preening of "the world's most exclusive club." Our ladies' lunch fell on hard times after Lesley Stahl moved away. She's such a good friend that she's willing to do the organizing, so we lazily count on her to visit Washington to get us all together again.

Now that we're among the older women in the workplace, we find we can make a difference for the younger women both personally and professionally, and that's very satisfying. Linda and Nina and I are such meddlers that we often try to arrange love lives as well as advise on work lives. Though we've had several successes, we've never been able to match our great triumph—now more than twenty-five years ago—when we arranged the introduction (subtle, we thought; not so subtle, she thought) of a younger friend of ours at NPR to Steve's brother Glenn. It worked! And my friend Kitty became my sister-in-law. Talk about a happy ending, especially for me.

It's important to have women with enough seniority and clout to be able to keep the bosses' feet to the fire, pointing out the absence of women in high places, or of opportunities for younger women. For years nobody did that better than my buddy Carole Simpson at ABC, but all of us old girls apply the pressure from time to time, though you still have to be careful not to push too hard or too often. Once ABC put a woman in charge of the Washington Bureau the place actually became somewhat sane—something no news organization's ever been accused of being in the past. It's remarkable how humor, sympathy, efficiency, and collegiality emanating from the top trickle down through an institution. But if it's made a difference for me to have Robin Sproul as my boss, I think she'd say that it made a difference for her to have people like Carole and me among her troops, speaking from long experience in the world of working-women, and also in the world of working moms. So many of the younger women came to us to counsel them on how to do it—how to strike the balance of work and family. For some, depending on their circumstances, the answer has been, you better take some time at home, the balance isn't working. Others take great hope from the fact that we've successfully raised girls who are working moms now themselves, at the same time that we were achieving professional success. Carole abandoned me a few years ago when she moved to Boston to provide some of that same advice, plus a pair of helping hands, to her own daughter.

Role models do matter, but so do plain old-fashioned, homey how-to suggestions. In the course of a day, I'll find myself going from an interview about the situation in Iraq to a conversation about a colleague's baby's tummy troubles. After a few times of hearing both me and the doctor say things like "Cheese, bananas, and rice," the young women stop bothering the doctor and just check in with the experienced mothers. It's a role, of course, that women have always played for one another—grandmothers, aunts, mothers, and mothers-in-law were on hand on the farm or in the village. As younger generations moved to the suburbs or away altogether, they lost or ignored the wisdom of older women, so Dr. Spock and his successors took over from Grandmother as child rearing became an occupation for "professionals." Ironically, it's in the thoroughly modern workplace where women of different generations are reconnecting.

When I learned the dreaded news heard by way too many women today—"You have breast cancer"—these women from all parts of my life supported me through the journey—and it *is* a journey, a long tough one from the time you get the diagnosis until the time you no longer wake up every morning in terror. (It was, of course, my husband who was the only one there to soothe me through that.) My cousins, my childhood friends, my college friends, my sisters-in-law, my friends from early days in Washington, from New York, from California, from Greece, and from my current work—everyone was in touch, propping me up, pushing me forward. Linda came with me to get my hair shaved once it started falling out, but that was a much less onerous assignment than the one I had asked of her earlier when she sat with me through the terrifying day of scans to see if the disease had spread any further than the nodes we knew it had invaded. That day, the person who was able to announce that, praise the Lord, the scans were clear was my oncologist, Joanne Zujewski, who is not only a world-class physician but a warm and funny friend. The fact of breast cancer forced me to a new level of friendship—one where I had to accept that I was the needy one. I had needed friends before, of course, especially in the horrific times when my father was lost and my sister died, and in the happy times when my kids got married, but this was different. This was my own death staring me in the face. But, along with my wonderful family, my friends came to the rescue.

Now, because my breast cancer was so public, I get calls all the time from women, or friends of women, or husbands of women who have just been diagnosed. I tell them to allow their friends in, to let their friends help. A different friend accompanied me for each of the chemotherapy sessions and it made such a difference in those long uncomfortable days to have someone to talk to and laugh with. Our lives are so busy that we don't often permit ourselves the enjoyment of whiling away a day with a good friend. Those treatments forced me to take that time. It's not something I would recommend—breast cancer—but it has widened my world of friends as I have come to know the doctors, nurses, and advocates in the field, and it has deepened my devotion to my old friends and family.

What's so special about these stories? Not a thing. Don't all friends have these experiences? Yes, that's the point. Women rely on friends. If you're lucky like me, you have a built-in best friend called a husband, but I will always need my female friends, and I think most women do. We simply can't exist without the connections to other women. That's where we draw sustenance and find safety. We can count on our women friends when we need a good laugh or a good cry. Women have always known this, as they found ways to cover vast distances in order to congregate—to share their tasks with other women on the pretense of efficiency, but, in fact, because we've known through the centuries that when we're together we have more fun.

Civil Rights Activist

■   ■   ■

"SO MANY PEOPLE ASK ME, 'HOW DO YOU DEAL WITH SO many different things?' But from my viewpoint, there was a central core to all of it. And if you follow it, really, it's always advancing women." That's what Dorothy Height's been doing for the last seventy-some years, ever since the 1930s when she organized young people in New York against lynching, and she's still doing it. She has not rested on her many laurels—the Presidential Medal of Freedom, the Congressional Gold Medal, the Presidential Citizens Medal, the highest honors bestowed on an American civilian. She continues to lead the National Council of Negro Women as chairman, twelve years after relinquishing her post as president.

Before stepping up from that job, Dr. Height secured a

spot on the famed "Avenue of Presidents" for the organization she had presided over for forty years. Dr. Height told me that when she bought the building, strategically located between the White House and the Capitol, it was the only one owned by African Americans in downtown Washington, D.C. She put together the financing for the historic old structure with a loan guaranteed by General Motors, Ford, and Chrysler. And though it was an effort to raise the money to pay for it, it was worth it because "our women's groups have been very conscious of the importance of having someplace you can claim as your own." Dorothy Height can claim that place of her own in history.

By the time Dr. Height achieved national notice as a leader in the civil rights movement, she was already a well-known figure here in Washington. My family cared deeply about civil rights; it had been a cause of consternation politically and morally all of our lives, and we knew many of the activists in the movement. But I also knew Dorothy Height because she and my mother had worked together on several projects—they were part of a cadre of women who seemed to run Washington. They ran welfare programs through Family and Child Services, they ran employment for the handicapped through Goodwill Industries, they established the first homes for abandoned and abused women in the House of Ruth. They used women's clubs to accomplish whatever social service program they thought was needed at that moment. Dorothy Height had been doing that ever since she was a little girl growing up in Rankin, Pennsylvania, where her father was a builder, her mother a private nurse.

It was at a time, early in the twentieth century, when the "women's club movement" was at its apex. In the decades after the Civil War, white women across the country organized to share common interests and community involvement. Under the leadership of activists like Ida B. Wells, black women soon followed suit, creating their own clubs. Some were devoted to study, many were devoted to service, all gave women the opportunity to work—and, presumably, gossip—together. (These societies were not always viewed as benign activities. When Julia Ward Howe established the New England Women's Club in 1868, the *Boston Transcript* editorialized that "Homes will be ruined, children neglected, woman is straying from her place." There was reason, in the end, to worry. Out of the club movement grew the suffrage movement, and we know what that did!)

Through her mother's affiliation with the Emma J. Moore Women's Club, Dorothy, in 1926 at the age of fourteen, became president of the Pennsylvania Girls' Clubs. Her whole childhood seems one of successes—she won a four-year college scholarship from the Elks for her oration on the Constitution—so it was not much of a surprise when Barnard College accepted her application for admission. What happened next, however, did surprise and sear Dorothy Height, wounding her in a way that still causes her to wince as she tells the story. She arrived at the Barnard dean's office, per instruction, and was kept waiting forever. Finally, she was told to come back in September because "we have a quota of two and we have two Negro students." Think of it, this fifteen-year-old sitting in a scary office in New York City, hearing something so humiliating. Shakily, decades later, Dr. Height told me the story. "Even as I tell it now, I can almost feel it. It was the most traumatic experience. I was afraid to get on the phone and call my mother." An older sister grabbed her by the hand, marched her to the subway and into the registration line at New York University. The dean there took one look at her grades and admitted her instantly. "Well, I tell you. To this moment I loved every moment at NYU," Dorothy Height declared with an appreciative chuckle.

First she studied religion until the head of the department told her, "You need to think of something else, because the church isn't ready for women. And the black church surely isn't ready for you." That's how Dorothy Height became a social worker, a relatively new line of work that had its origins in the settlement house movement, which had grown out of the women's clubs. She finished NYU in three years and got her master's degree in the fourth; then she did more graduate work at Columbia University. Next stop, far from the world of academe: the Brownsville Community Center, in Brooklyn's highest-delinquency area. Then, she recalled, "I was recruited by the Department of Welfare, the City of New York, to join that staff. And I left the Brownsville Center because I couldn't resist twenty-seven fifty a week." After that, it was a job at the Young Women's Christian Association, and it was for life.

Dr. Height told the story as if it happened yesterday. She was the new staffer at the Harlem Y, so she drew weekend duty. The assignment: escort First Lady Eleanor Roosevelt to a meeting called by Mary McLeod Bethune. So it was that the twenty-five-year-old Dorothy met two of the twentieth century's most influential women. It was November 7, 1937, she said, "and as I was leaving, Mrs. Bethune stopped me, and she asked my name. And I told her. And then she said, 'Come back. We need you.' So, I've been back ever since." Back as a worker for the National Council of Negro Women, an organization then headed by Mrs. Bethune, who was part of President Roosevelt's "Black Cabinet" advising him on minorities. Two years earlier, educator Mary McLeod Bethune, the daughter of former slaves, had organized the council as a coalition of 28 black women's groups. (Today 39 national and 240 community-based organizations, representing 4 million women, fall under the NCNW umbrella.) Dorothy Height found herself working with the council as a volunteer while doing her paid work for the YWCA, where she moved on to the national staff in 1944.

Her two roles meshed, because the Y was a remarkably progressive organization. Modern women's histories include lines like "The YWCA was not integrated until 1946." To me the fact that the Y *did* integrate in 1946 is mind-boggling.

Remember the time—separation of the races was legally enforced throughout the South and informally observed in much of the rest of the country; soldiers fighting in World War II did so in segregated units; it was eight years before *Brown v. Board of Education* ordered desegregation of the public schools, two years before a civil rights plank was added to the platform of the Democratic Party. Still, in a brave move, the Y decided that to be true to its Christian principles it must endorse equality of the races. The staff, with the assistance of Dorothy Height, helped write the interracial charter the YWCA convention in 1946 would be called upon to adopt. As the meeting was set to convene, she recalled, 210 associations resisted the idea of integration, saying, "Given our Christian purpose, it's a thing we should do. But if we do it, we will go out of existence in our community. We will have no white members."

Trying to give some sense of the drama, Dr. Height recounted the lobbying of the various Y chapters by the leadership, and the stirring keynote address by Dr. Benjamin Mays, then president of Morehouse College, an all-black institution: "'I hear you say that the time is not ripe. But the time is always ripe to do justice. And if you have a Christian purpose, if the time is not ripe, then it should be your purpose to ripen the time.' It's hard to recapture what happened. Some women from some southern communities walked out. Some left the convention. They said they could not hold their heads up if they stayed and were there for the action." But the charter was adopted, and when she told me the story Dr. Height could still hear the president of the organization, as she looked out over the group of three thousand women, asking, " 'Is this going to be easy to do?' And there was a kind of 'No,' as if it had been organized. But that was the turning point. And the YWCA kept moving. And I think one of the things that was so encouraging to me was the leadership of women."

If it was hard to get the women of the YWCA to accept racial equality, it turned out to be even harder to get the men of the civil rights movement to accept women's equality. As the president of the National Council of Negro Women, a post she assumed in 1957, Dorothy Height took her place at the table of the black organizations. (The others and their presidents: the Urban League, Whitney Young; the NAACP, Roy Wilkins; the Student Nonviolent Coordinating Committee, John Lewis; the Southern Christian Leadership Conference, Martin Luther King, Jr.; the Congress of Racial Equality, James Farmer; the Brotherhood of Sleeping Car Porters, A. Philip Randolph.) At almost every movement meeting she was the only woman in the room. When they began organizing the massive 1963 March on Washington, she started militating for a woman speaker. But she failed: "It was impossible. We did everything. Their arguments were very clear. 'Women are represented in the NAACP. Women are in the Urban League. Women belong to the churches. Women are in the labor movement. Women are represented.' Here were great champions of justice, and they would say,

'Well, you know how highly we regard you.'" To show their "regard," the men gave the women choice seats for the march; they could be seen but not heard. "The only female voice heard was Mahalia Jackson. And we kept saying, 'We're fighting against this.' I said, 'Everybody thinks that Negroes can sing. But also we want to be able to speak up for ourselves.'" Finally, the women dropped the argument: "We just hit a point where we just had to ride above it because it was so important not to have a great division."

The experience served to reinforce a lesson already all too well learned—that women would have to help themselves. And self-help has been the hallmark of the many programs initiated by the NCNW. Basic hunger needed to be addressed, particularly in the Deep South, and the organization came up with an inventive way to make a difference—pig banks. Starting with fifty-five Yorkshire pigs, families in Sunflower County, Mississippi, were able to become self-sustaining. As part of the program sponsored by the council, experts went to Mississippi to tend to the health of the pigs, and they ended up serving the families as well—teaching them about preventive medicine, good eating habits, and hygiene. Something as simple as pigs led to better medical care and education for those families. It's hard to imagine a group of men being willing to operate on so humble a scale. (Now, ironically, it's obesity among black children that the council is concentrating on, working on a project with the National Institutes of Health.)

The self-help theme also underlies the Black Family Reunions that Dorothy Height's organization started in 1986. They bring together black Americans in cities all over the country to enjoy one another's company, good food, and good music, and also to learn about health, home ownership, and higher education. After ten years of pulling together those reunions, Dr. Height marveled, "It has been amazing; over that period we've had some fourteen million people in eight cities without a single police incident." The idea for the reunions, which now have been successfully bringing people together for twenty-four years, came from Dorothy Height's childhood: "The emphasis is on traditional values and on our coping skills and helping people get a sense of stressing the community as more of an extended family. That's what supported many of us as we were growing up, the fact that everybody in the community looked out for you." The community looked out for the children because the parents, mother and father, were at work. Dorothy Height has always found all of this agonizing in the white community about working outside the home a little silly. When she served on President Kennedy's Commission on the Status of Women, she had to remind her white sisters that their experiences were not universal. "I remember that as we were coming down to our conclusions that said something like 'Women grow up, become adolescents, go into the labor force, get married, come out of the labor force and have their children, go back in the labor force.' And I said, 'That sounds to me like another world. That's not the African-American woman.'"

Black women worked for pay and they worked for free, taking on double duty in the workforce and the volunteer force, plus, of course, the home force. With some indignation Dr. Height insisted, "There's a myth that we don't volunteer. We've only survived because we volunteer. We have provided for ourselves so much that our white sisters take for granted. I remember when I worked at the Harlem Y. After a year, I was put in charge of the residence. There was not a bed in the city of New York in 1938 for a black unwed mother. Yet we had Florence Crittenden Homes [for white unwed mothers] all over the city. Those little club groups, they provided those services." Little club groups like those her mother had been part of, and those she had known as a girl, then used as an adult—those were the social service agencies blacks had to depend on.

They still do, many through programs initiated by the NCNW. But Dorothy Height still feels a great urgency to do more: "The fastest-growing entries into the correction system now are girls, a 23 percent increase. And many who are incarcerated have two to three children. So, I think that much more attention needs to be given. That's why we put the stress on the family. I'm not saying we don't need to put stress on the black male, but we need a stress on our young women as well. They are the ones who are left with the families. So, I think we have to use every strategy that we can to reinforce those who are trying to make it. There are so many who are underachieving because of their frustration. They don't see a life for themselves. That's why I think that we have to offer every opportunity, every incentive, to encourage our young women."

By doing that, Dr. Height's convinced, the whole society will prosper, even though men don't believe it. Looking back over her many years in the fray, she says emphatically, "The advances of women have always advanced men." A prime example: a case in the Philadelphia post office, where women couldn't lift the heavy bags, so men said the women shouldn't have the jobs. "Men shouldn't have been lifting them either," she recalled with a laugh, "they had hernias and all from it. We said, 'If you can put a man on the moon, there ought to be some way to lift those.' Well, they got ways of electronically doing that. That advanced it for men. And I think a lot of men don't understand that." There's an understatement.

Dorothy Height has spent a lifetime understating and conciliating and getting things done, constantly pushing the ball forward, and finally winning the recognition the men in the civil rights movement would not grant her back in 1963. President Ronald Reagan gave her the Presidential Citizens Medal in 1989, the same year she won the Franklin Delano Roosevelt Freedom Medal. Then President Clinton in 1994 awarded her, along with Rosa Parks, the Presidential Medal of Freedom. Probably thinking that was the pinnacle, in

2003, at the age of ninety-one, she published her memoir, *Open Wide the Freedom Gates.* But there was still more to come. On her ninety-second birthday in 2004, President George W. Bush traveled to the Capitol to honor her as the recipient of the Congressional Gold Medal, and Nancy Pelosi, the woman who would become the first female Speaker of the House, stood to thank her: "At a time when women were overlooked and underappreciated, Dr. Height was often the only woman at the table. During one meeting of the White House civil rights panel, she took a seat next to President Lyndon Johnson. When a male member of the council insisted on having that, she was ushered down the line. But Dr. Height was never one to be pushed aside. She pulled up a chair and sat down on the other side of President Johnson. And because she did, that day the whole world saw an African American woman seated proudly next to the President of the United States. As they do today." What the whole world saw there in historic Statuary Hall was Dorothy Height, elegant as always, crowned by one of her signature hats, seated by the president, surrounded by the bronze and marble replicas of famous men. If only that admissions officer at Barnard could see her now.

But, of course, another surprise was still in store for Dorothy Height. After all of her years of toiling for civil rights, at the age of ninety-six she saw a black man elected president of the United States. That night she was at the National Council of Negro Women's headquarters on Pennsylvania Avenue. "I cannot even describe to you what happened when that final word came over. It just exploded, everybody was so excited," she told National Public Radio two days later. "I'm so glad I lived to see it." But this eternally optimistic woman insisted that she had always believed it would happen, that she wasn't concerned that in the end white people wouldn't vote for an African American. Why was she so confident? "I worked with many white women who took a strong stand, but they didn't discuss it at home because their husbands didn't agree with them. Now the YWCA has 'empower women and eliminate racism' as its slogan." She had seen change. And she was on hand to see it up close on January 20, 2009. As Barack Obama stood before the west front of the Capitol to take the oath of office as President of the United States, there on the platform with him, erectly in her wheelchair, sat Dorothy Height. She had worked her whole life so that this day could happen, and she had the support of an entire sisterhood. As she told me years ago when she reflected back on her many days in the trenches: "We had strong leadership among men. But I think that women when they get on something, we don't give up easily." Lord knows she hasn't.

R EPORTER

OUTSIDE OF THE SENATE FAMILY GALLERY HANGS AN OLD OIL
painting depicting the meeting of the Electoral Commission
of 1876, assembled in the Senate Chamber to decide the
validity of ballots in the presidential election. Women fill
the press gallery in the picture, and a guide on an adjoining
wall conveniently identifies each of them, with the newspapers they represented. Why, I wondered aloud one day, were
there more women in the press gallery in 1876 than in 1976?
By 1996, when I was asking this question, women were beginning to fill the places again. The guard who overheard
me answered, "Because they could write." Well, sure, they
could write in 1976, too, but not many papers gave them
the chance. Then the guard patiently explained that it wasn't

creative writing he was talking about, it was handwriting. Woman practiced better penmanship than men, so those elegant-looking ladies in the press gallery were essentially stenographers, not reporters. What a disappointment!

That experience set me off on a little expedition into history, in an attempt to learn more about the women journalists who came before me. And what an eye-opener it turned out to be, starting with the story of Mary Katherine Goddard, publisher of the *Maryland Journal*. Though she produced the big scoop on the battle of Bunker Hill, she's come down through history for her printing rather than her reporting. We all know that the Declaration of Independence was approved on July 4, 1776, but it took a while for the revolutionaries to get up the courage to sign their names to the incendiary document, and a while longer to publish and promulgate it. By the time Congress ordered the distribution of the Declaration, in January 1777, the British had put prices on the patriots' heads and run them out of Philadelphia and into Baltimore. There they took the printing job to the leading newspaper publisher, Mary Katherine Goddard. Printers normally affixed their initials to their work, much the way a union "bug" might mark a document today, but understanding the significance, and the danger, of what she was doing, Goddard signed her full name as the printer of the Declaration of Independence. That copy of the document, with her name boldly appended, is now in the Library of Congress.

Out of seventy-eight papers in the American colonies, sixteen were edited by women. We haven't come anywhere near that percentage since then. Some of those early women writers were already on their soapboxes—advocating equal education for women, railing against corruption in high places. One of them, Anne Newport Royall, called the "Grandma of Muckrakers" by a biographer, was actually convicted in 1829 of the crime of being a "common scold." Can you imagine if such a charge existed today? We'd all be in trouble. A couple of newspapermen paid her ten-dollar fine to preserve "the honor of the press." The most famous story about Anne Newport Royall might be too good to be true. Desperate for an interview with President John Quincy Adams, the story goes, she caught him swimming in the Potomac River and sat on his clothes until he agreed to talk. The thought of the thoroughly priggish Adams shivering in his birthday suit before this somewhat wild newspaperwoman gives me such a giggle that I certainly hope it did happen.

Some of the nineteenth-century women in journalism became household names. Mary E. Clemmer Ames (they all seemed to have multiple names) wrote a weekly "Woman's Letter from Washington" for the *New York Independent* and then the *Brooklyn Daily Union*. In 1869, her last year at the Brooklyn paper, she made the princely sum of five thousand dollars. (Almost one hundred years later, when I was working in New York on a business newsletter, my salary wasn't much more than that.) Most famous of all was Nellie Bly (born Elizabeth Jane Cochran) who started working at the *Pittsburgh Dispatch* when she was either eighteen or twenty-one—she seems to have been accurate about almost everything but her age. The paper hired her after she sent a well-written letter to the editor supporting women's rights. But her fame came as an investigative reporter for the *New York World* when she feigned insanity to get into the asylum on Blackwell's Island in order to expose the abuses there. The episode serves as a forerunner of today's hidden-camera controversies. To capitalize on her notoriety, in 1889 the *World* sponsored a contest challenging Nellie Bly to go around the world in fewer than Phileas Fogg's eighty days. Readers guessed exactly how long it would take her, and almost a million people submitted entries. The answer: seventy-two days, six hours, eleven minutes, and fourteen seconds for a trip by ship, train, horse, and burro. Brass bands, fireworks, and parades accompanied her special train from San Francisco to New York, the last leg of her journey. The whole country knew Nellie Bly, and cared enough to come out to cheer her on. Her celebrity certainly outdistanced that of any television star today.

Over thirty-six years Nellie Bly wrote more than six hundred newspaper articles, including her coverage of World War I from the eastern front. Since she stayed in Vienna even after the United States entered the war, appealing through her articles for aid to Austrian war widows and orphans, she was investigated by U.S. military intelligence as a possible enemy agent. The conclusion: "She is outspoken in her opinions going to the extent of being aggressive and defiant." Her great sin, it seems, was attempting to warn the Allies about the dangers of Bolshevism. When she returned to New York after the war, the *Evening Journal* hired her as an advice columnist. But the swashbuckling reporter didn't let that change of assignment dampen her reformist spirit—her slice of the newspaper soon evolved into a sort of social service clearinghouse, a place for her to badger the authorities on behalf of her readers.

While Nellie Bly was filing daily stories from her round-the-world adventure, Ida B. Wells was busy acquiring a share of the *Memphis Free Speech and Headlight*. It was a small paper, and this fiery young woman, who had been born a slave, was ready to use part of her salary as a schoolteacher to buy into it. She had already contributed many articles on racial injustice to journals around the country, under the pseudonym "Iola." Now she used her own byline, and her newspaper accounts of poor school conditions for black children got her fired from the job. That was nothing compared to her anti-lynching campaign, which resulted in a white mob storming the *Free Speech* offices and destroying the presses. Wells, who was in New York at the time, was warned never to return to Memphis. Undeterred, she kept writing, selling the *Free Speech*'s circulation list for part ownership of the *New York Age*. She attacked white male "chivalry" with her scathing, "No one who reads the record, as it is written on the faces of the million mulattoes in the South, will for a minute conceive that the southern white man had a very chivalrous regard for the honor due women of his race or respect for the womanhood which circumstances placed in his power." Her crusade against lynching took her on a European lecture tour, where she learned about female civic institutions. When she returned to America, Wells left the newspaper business behind her, taking her crusade for justice into politics, where she organized the first black women's suffrage organization and was one of the founders of the NAACP.

By insisting that only women journalists could cover her press conferences, Eleanor Roosevelt did a lot to promote their position; then the lead-up to World War II and the war itself brought women to a more prominent place in the press corps. But it was a struggle the whole way. Anne O'Hare McCormick, the first woman to serve on the *New York Times* editorial board, wrote most of her groundbreaking reports as a freelancer because the *Times* publisher just couldn't bring himself to put her on staff. Hers is a remarkable story. Her father abandoned his wife and three daughters, leaving her mother to support the family by running a dry-goods store and going door-to-door selling poetry, of all things. Somehow she managed to send Anne to college and gave her the grounding for a job as associate editor of the *Catholic Universe Bulletin*. After Anne O'Hare married, she accompanied her husband on his many business trips and started sending back reports on what she observed to the *New York Times*. Though the paper readily printed her dispatches, Arthur Ochs refused to hire her, saying, "We have almost a prohibition against women on our editorial staff." So her famous interviews with Hitler, Stalin, Mussolini, and Roosevelt, her warnings about the rise of Fascism, all appeared as the work of a freelance reporter. When Ochs died, the *Times* finally put her on the payroll at the age of fifty-six. The next year, 1937, Anne O'Hare McCormick became the first woman writing for a major newspaper to win the prestigious Pulitzer Prize. (A woman student had previously won the prize in a onetime only award to a student newspaper.)

The great World War II correspondent Helen Kirkpatrick faced similar problems getting hired on the home front. After she graduated from college in 1931, the editor of the *New York Herald Tribune* gave her a bleak assessment of career prospects for women in journalism, so she went to work at Macy's instead. (The *Current Biography* of 1941 calls work at the department store "often a temporary stopover for bright college graduates.") After a few years there, she returned to the field she had studied in college—international relations— and took a job in Geneva, Switzerland, with the Foreign Policy Association. There she started writing, and newspapers started printing what she wrote. She became influential on the American lecture circuit, wrote a book, then moved to London, where she published a weekly news digest read by all the British leaders. Even after all of this, and another weighty book, she was told by the publisher of the *Chicago*

Daily News that he didn't hire women for the foreign desk. "I can't change my sex, but you can change your policy," she told him, and he did. Her first story as a staffer in 1939: an interview with the Duke of Windsor, something her male colleagues claimed couldn't be done; the duke would not talk to the press. As World War II heated up, Kirkpatrick filed three and four times a day for a column syndicated in twenty-four newspapers. Her war coverage, including her vivid descriptions of the London blitz, became so popular that the *Daily News* plastered her picture on their trucks to lure more readers to the paper. When Edward R. Murrow tried to add her to his band of war correspondents, CBS News told him no more women, so he took on cub reporter Charles Collingwood instead. The only woman to serve on the correspondents' committee planning coverage of the Normandy invasion, Helen Kirkpatrick crossed France with the French Second Armored Division and set up a news bureau in Paris. At war's end she covered the Nuremberg trials from her position as the *New York Post*'s European correspondent. Then, at age forty-five, and probably exhausted, she got married and retired.

Many women reporters didn't have a choice about retiring. After the war they found themselves in a "Rosie the Reporter" situation—forced to give up their jobs when the men came home. One was Dorothy Jurney, the assistant city editor of the *Washington News,* who was told in 1946 to train a cub reporter, a returning soldier, to replace her. She moved to Miami, where she resigned herself to abandoning hard news for the women's pages. But she soon found that she was able to have a good deal of impact there by covering such issues as housing needs in the black community. A move to the *Detroit Free Press* as the women's editor gave her more opportunities to assign stories on women's pension rights, women professors' tenure battles, and women as political candidates. Reporters around the country started using the women's pages for serious topics, so newspapers shifted gears, stopped separating out news for women, and started calling the sections "Style" or "Living," so that serious news affecting women effectively disappeared. When an editor of the *New York Times* was called on this question several years ago, he justified the absence of women from his news columns by saying, "We don't cover tea parties." The women of the *Times* instantly had a campaign-style pin made that showed a teapot with a slash through it. It's been on my office wall ever since.

After World War II, some war correspondents stayed on. Most notably, Pauline Frederick, who had been advised by a boss to "stay away from radio, it doesn't like women." Fortunately, she ignored him, and NBC liked her indeed. But it was for the North American Newspaper Alliance that she covered the war and the Nuremberg trials, and then she went to ABC, where she appeared as the first woman news reporter on television at the 1948 Democratic Convention. Later, back at NBC, her renown grew with her regular program, *Pauline Frederick Reporting,* and as the United Nations correspondent. In 1976 she was picked as the first woman to moderate a televised presidential debate. Finally, she wrote news analysis for National Public Radio. There she was, this icon, and I would see her in the ladies' room!

I have had the privilege of knowing and working with a good many of the women who battled in this business until the law finally took their side. Nancy Dickerson, the first female TV correspondent for CBS, could not have been kinder to me in the 1960s when I was just starting out and she was one of the most powerful people in Washington. The women of the *New York Times,* Nan Robertson and Eileen Shanahan and Maggie Hunter, were my husband's colleagues but my heroines. They took on the Great Gray Lady of the *Times* in a suit that embarrassed the paper into paying attention to its women—its correspondents, its secretaries, its women workers at every level. (Before their lawsuit, one of Washington's great reporters, Mary McGrory, had been told by the *Times* bureau chief that she would be asked to work on the switchboard if she worked there.) Women at *Newsweek* and *Time* took similar chances suing their bosses, to the benefit of all the women who came after them.

Women fighting for an equal place in journalism also battled the journalistic cliques that hung out Male Only signs. Back in 1868 journalist Jane Cunningham Croly organized the newspaperwomen's society Sororis after she had been barred from a New York Press Club dinner. Things hadn't changed one iota a hundred years later at the National Press Club. No female members were accepted, and women covering events there were forced to stew and sweat together in the balcony while the men sat in air-conditioned comfort in the room below, enjoying a meal. It was not until 1971, after much organized agitation, that people of my sex were admitted as full members.

We women correspondents owe eternal debts of gratitude to the women who pitched fits in print journalism, and the women in broadcasting like Marlene Sanders and Barbara Walters who went before us. It must have been incredibly difficult for them, because it was plenty tough for me when I was starting out—male bosses told me how women couldn't broadcast news because our voices weren't authoritative enough, how women couldn't be writers at newsmagazines because men would have to work for us, how women couldn't be counted on to stay in a job because we would go off and have babies. It's important to understand that when this was happening to me and to other women my age, we had no idea it was happening to anyone else, as it was in almost every profession. I'm sure some of my contemporaries understood that we were being wildly discriminated against, but it took me and—I've learned in later years—my good friends a while to get it.

I remember it so well. After college I had gotten a job through the placement office—no kidding. A family of

Wellesley women, headed by the indomitable Sophie Altman, produced a series of TV shows out of Washington. They hired me to help with the main production, *It's Academic,* a high school quiz show that's still thriving in Washington. Local versions of the program aired around the country, and as the show was picked up by more stations, I helped produce it in the new cities. Mrs. Altman had also for many years produced a program on the local NBC station called *Teen Talk,* which, coincidentally, I had appeared on as a teenager. While I was working there, the station decided that the show had run its course, but the managers still wanted Altman Productions to come up with another public service program to fulfill its licensing requirements. The solution: a program that brought the huge community of foreign correspondents in Washington onto the public airwaves and in touch with American public officials. It was called *Meeting of the Minds,* and I was its anchor. I was twenty-one. Of course I had never done anything like it before, but I think I was too young and dumb to be scared, and the guests and journalists treated me well—after all, they wanted to be on TV. As the program that preceded the old standby *Meet the Press,* it was watched by all of official Washington.

My good friend Roger Wilkins, the civil rights leader and historian, tells a funny story about that. He served as assistant attorney general in the Johnson administration, but for some reason LBJ had gotten it in his head that Wilkins might be in Bobby Kennedy's camp, which to Johnson was the ultimate disloyalty. Roger appeared as a guest on my program and performed a masterful defense of Johnson's civil rights record. The president saw the show and from there on out Roger was always in his good graces.

When I finally convinced Steven to marry me it never occurred to me to try to keep my job, even though I was making more money than he was. I, without thinking twice about it, just said good-bye and headed to New York, where he was working. Then I started looking. And I was appalled. Men were so blatant in their "We don't hire women" statements—one of them even delivered that Olympian judgment with his hand on my thigh—that it was truly shocking. But there was no one to share the shock. Steven didn't think what I was telling him was particularly odd; the world for men and women had never been the same, why would it be now? He probably thought I was exaggerating anyway. All he knew for sure was that I kept failing to snare employment. Fortunately, I couldn't type or take shorthand. Many women of my era graduated from fine schools like Wellesley, Smith, and Vassar and then went on to secretarial school at Katherine Gibbs. It was my view that learning clerical skills could stick you forever in a clerical job. I know people for whom that hasn't been true, but I also know plenty for whom it has. I will never advise a young woman even in this day and age to "come in the door" as a secretary. Everybody needs secretaries so desperately that a person good at it is trapped, a person bad at it is branded as a lousy worker.

At one point in this job search, I lost my temper. It was clear I had nothing to lose; the man interviewing me thought I was speaking Swahili when I suggested that women might, in fact, be writers for his newsmagazine. He kept talking to me about all the female researchers and what great jobs they did and how much they loved it there. (I was not even slightly a feminist at this point, but I had been raised in the South and I knew an "Our servants are so close, they are actually members of our family" statement when I heard one.) I allowed as how I thought my credentials went beyond researcher status and that men who had graduated in my year from comparable schools were thriving at his magazine. He was so chagrined by this conversation that he didn't know how to deal with it; I was challenging his eternal verities. Men did one thing, women did another. What was the problem? Many, many years later this man was up for an important job at NPR when I had become someone who could make a difference in his employment. I didn't think he had any memory whatsoever of our long-ago conversation, and I didn't rat on him to the search committee. I decided they could figure out on their own that he was not the right person for our organization.

When I finally did get a job writing for a weekly newsletter, I loved it. Reporting is, after all, a license to snoop, and you get paid to learn something new every day and then tell the world about it. It's not necessarily the most mature of vocations, with its instant gratification of being able to see your story in the paper, hear and see your broadcast on radio and TV on a daily basis, but it is fun. Before we moved to Greece in 1974, I went around to the networks asking them to use me if they could, saying that I was studying the language and would have access to Steve's telex machine. Everyone expressed some interest; CBS actually gave me a tape recorder to take with me. I planned to get the family settled and then start pitching stories. Well, no sooner had we moved into our house and placed the kids in schools than war broke out in Cyprus. Steve was summoned to the island, where he was frighteningly out of touch for several days. By the time he came home I was a seasoned radio reporter, filing every hour. I had even learned to rely on my five-year-old son as a source: He had counted the number of tanks heading up the main avenue out of Athens. On the day the military regime fell and democracy returned to Greece, my report, which I filed from a flower stall outside the presidential palace, led the *CBS Evening News*. Finally, there could be no question that I had well and truly broken into journalism.

When I returned to Washington, the world had changed in the eleven years since I had left. Women were in a considerably better position. And at National Public Radio women were in prime positions. Part of the reason for that was the pay scale, that is, low. It was easier to get good women to work for low wages than good men. Also, the network started from scratch in 1970, so there weren't men already in place who would have to be replaced if women were hired to cover such subjects as the Supreme Court and Congress and candidates. People often ask me whether I have trouble getting interviews because I am a woman. As far as I know, the answer to that question is no. Politicians care much more about the initials after your name—NPR, ABC—than the letters before it—Mr. or Ms. I've always joked that a news organization with a wide enough circulation could send a two-headed monster to interview a politician and the only response would be, "Would you like a cup of coffee, or perhaps two cups?" They know my interviews will be seen and heard by millions of people, even if I am wearing a skirt.

At some point, being a woman became an advantage, at least for some of us. When women viewers and listeners and readers started objecting to the all-white-male casts of characters presented to them on program after program, the tables turned. Producers and editors actively looked for women for their broadcasts and broadsheets. Or at least they looked for one woman. That would do it. Nina Totenberg tells the story of having an editor tell her, "But, Nina, we already have our woman." ABC News would probably never have come looking for me had I been a man. The network thought it needed a woman, at least occasionally, on the roundtable at the end of the Brinkley program. The producers had tried a few but hadn't settled on anyone, so someone suggested me and it worked. But it wasn't because I was a woman that ten years later I ended up as the coanchor of the broadcast.

To hear many men tell it, women are getting all the jobs, taking them away from the people to whom they naturally belong, men. Baloney. Usually we still find ourselves fighting, if not to get in, at least to move up. How often have you seen a TV program where everyone on it is a woman? I must say, it really ticks me off when someone says, "Oh, she only got that job because she's a woman," as Washington wags did when Madeleine Albright became the first female secretary of state. Talk about no-win situations. You spend the first half of your working life being told you can't have a job because you're a woman and the second half being told you only got the job because you're a woman. Give me a break! (Condoleezza Rice faced none of the same snide comments, and by the time Hillary Clinton came along people started asking if the job was uniquely suited to women. People really are funny.)

Now some of the women who went through the experience of being shut out of the good jobs have reached high positions in the work world. But we all remember what we went through, and how our experiences changed the landscape. Katharine Graham revealed in her wonderful book that she had trouble as a woman, even though she was the *boss,* the publisher of the *Washington Post.* It was when women started sharing the stories of our struggles that the modern women's movement got its momentum. We went into the workplace as a group, an entire generation of educated women that was determined to break down barriers for ourselves and the women who came after us, and we have the scratches and bruises to show for it. But it mattered. It mattered for us as individuals and it also mattered to the institutions we infiltrated to hear women's voices.

Take journalism as an example. Look at the things women wrote about—remember Nellie Bly highlighting the problems of divorce and slum life and the plight of war widows and orphans and ending her journalistic days with a social services column. None of the men writing at the time noticed, as Anne O'Hare McCormick did, that after two world wars in Europe more women had survived than men and women were left to clean up the mess. McCormick campaigned for more female representation at the San Francisco Conference that established the United Nations. And then there were Dorothy Jurney and her contemporaries who used the women's pages to underline women's problems. It's still happening today. Women journalists write more about women politicians and issues affecting families and children, whether it's breast cancer research or hardships in child care or overcrowding in schools. A recent study showed what any woman in a newsroom could tell you—women promote stories that connect more to readers and viewers, and that try to get people involved in the community.

We also brought a different sensibility to political reporting, for better or for worse. When there were only "boys on the bus," male reporters covering male candidates for office, no one ever considered a politician's behavior toward women relevant to his ability to do the job. When women joined the campaign caravans, they did think it made a difference. Gary Hart's peccadilloes were something women in newsrooms kept puzzling over. How could we deal with it? We thought it mattered, but there were no road maps for this kind of coverage. Then Hart made it easy by throwing down the gauntlet to follow him, and the *Miami Herald* did. And then there was Bill Clinton and Monica Lewinsky. Enough said. A lot of people are sorry that we now know so much about a president's or a presidential candidate's private life. I'm not among them. I think character counts, especially for the chief executive, who serves in a singular position, who does not have the check of 99 other senators or 434 other members of the House. And I think that attitudes toward women and family contribute to the definition of character.

It's taken many decades for the "girls on the bus" to move into anchor seats and major decision-making positions in journalism. But it's beginning to happen. Both of the news organizations I work for are now headed by women—Anne Sweeney at ABC and Vivian Schiller at NPR. And there is finally a solo woman anchor of a network evening news broadcast—though Katie Couric has taken her lumps. Women are also on the mastheads of major newspapers—including the *Washington Post,* where Katharine Graham's granddaughter Katharine Weymouth is following in her grandmother's gutsy footsteps. But still, if you turn on your TV set for the evening news, you would never know that white men make up only 36 percent of the electorate. You would think it's the rest of us who are in the minority. Despite the fact that two-thirds of the students in American journalism schools are women, white men still fill the prime slots in both broadcasting and print. A 2006 survey showed that women reported only 28 percent of the major stories on network news, minorities only 15 percent. At newspapers, where the pay is not as good, the numbers are somewhat better but still not great. The American Society of Newspaper Editors' most recent census counts women as 39 percent of the writers/reporters and 35 percent of the "supervisors." The numbers for minorities: 14 percent of the reporters, 11 percent of the supervisors.

Without diversity in newsrooms—without people of different ages, races, sexes, and interests—some ideas, some aspects of community life never come to the table, and the country is poorer for their absence. Though it's a very different journalistic world than the one I started out in more than forty years ago, it's still not reflective of the world we live in. To give a true picture of the country, we need more diversity in boardrooms where the bottom-line decisions are made. Don't hold your breath.

MECHANIC, FIRST CLASS

▨   ▨   ▨

"I'M A MECHANIC, FIRST CLASS." I WISH I COULD ADE-quately describe the breadth and brightness of the smile on Eva Oliver's face as she said those words. They represented the fulfillment of an incredible struggle up out of welfare and into the successful pursuit of the American dream.

This conversation with Eva Oliver took place in the cheery house she built with her own hands on an acre of land just outside Baton Rouge, Louisiana. I first met her in Washington where she had traveled to receive an award from the National Commission on Working Women, and when I heard the outlines of her story I knew that I wanted to learn more about her. My chance came when the producers of *This Week with David Brinkley* told the program's participants that we could each interview anyone we wanted for the Christmas broadcast. What an opportunity! On a television show watched religiously by Washington policy makers, I could actually talk at some length to someone their decisions directly affected.

The bare facts were these: At the age of thirty, with two tiny children, Eva Oliver, welfare recipient, enrolled in a state-sponsored training program that placed her in a job at Allied Signal, now Honeywell, a huge chemical company in Baton Rouge. She had moved up in the job to the position of first-class mechanic, the first African American woman to achieve that status. One of her children was in college, another ready to join the military to pay for her college education. Ms. Oliver had moved out of her dangerous city neighborhood to an area of fenced-in yards, friendly neighbors, and fine vegetable gardens. She had built her own house in the evenings and on weekends when she wasn't performing a backbreaking job at Allied. In her spare time she counseled women on welfare.

The bare facts were impressive enough, but I knew that the full story of this tough, capable lady had to be truly interesting. So the camera crew and I arrived on Eva Oliver's doorstep a little before Christmas Day 1994. And we listened to Ms. Oliver, a tall, open-faced woman, ready with a big laugh or a big hug, tell her tale.

"I did the welfare thing, I drew unemployment, I did a day's work anywhere I could get a day's work because I had to survive. Then you turn around and you make mistakes in your life and you get to where you made so many that they all stack up. And life is about making good choices. That's number one. Please, God, make good choices in your life. And if you make the bad choices and you get down to the bottom, then you have to do something about it."

The something that Eva Oliver did was listen to a minister who kept coming around asking her what she was doing and kept urging her to go to the state's Office of Women's Services. She'd agree but never follow through. Finally, the minister gave her the name and number of someone there, and Ms. Oliver called and explained that she wanted to work in a plant, where she knew the pay was good, but she had no training whatsoever. The state agent gave her the information that they were starting a training program for blue-collar women, and Eva Oliver applied for the class. She was rejected. Despite the discouragement she had the guts to press on. "I went down to see them and I told her, 'I'm not going to take no for an answer.' So they sent the head of the program down and I told him, 'This is no joke for me. I have two kids. I can't get a job. I need some training. I don't know what else to do. Can you-all please help me?' And he said, 'Because of your determination, if anybody fails the physical, I'll let you know.'" Two days later he called and said, "You're in."

It was a training program that paid students the minimum wage while they were in school. That, combined with her mother's and sisters' willingness to care for the kids, made it possible for Eva Oliver to get the skills she needed, and she went from being the last person accepted into the class to the first one hired out of it. Getting the job turned out to be the easy part. The hard part was doing it. She remembers with a laugh how terrified she was standing over a bubbling acid pit in nearly one-hundred-degree heat, digging holes. "I took this little shovel and I stood out there and I dug and I dug and I dug. And I prayed the whole time. I said, 'Oh, God, please, Jesus, let me handle this. I got insurance on my kids and I'm going to be able to take care of myself. I can't lose this. Please, Lord, help me.' And I dug those six holes. It took me a week to do it, but I dug those six holes. And at the end I said, 'Why, thank you, God.' And I think I realized that you can do anything you put your mind to. And that worked out, because after I got my first paycheck I said, 'I don't care where it's at, I'll be there.' "

Listening to Eva Oliver talk about what a "scary experience" it was for her to go for the first time into a plant, I could almost feel along with her the sense of being overwhelmed by pipes and wires, almost smell the acid pit as she described it. It made me a little suspicious about what was going on there. Were they testing her, seeing if the woman was up to the job? "I think they wanted to know right off hand does she want to turn and run at the first hard thing that comes along. I think they wanted to know right off hand would she stand it." And, she added, the men worried about their own security. Did women coming into the plant mean women would take their jobs? They eventually settled into an uneasy truce, with what she calls just a little hassling here and there. "Sometimes emotion with women will come up. And you run to the bathroom and you do your little crying and then you wipe your eyes and come back out. But it was hard. And for me it wasn't a choice."

That's the theme Eva Oliver struck over and over again. For her it wasn't a choice. She had to do this work. It was her way out, her salvation. From what? From welfare. "Collecting a check from the state is a trap as far as I see it. I wanted better. I didn't want to be dependent on anybody. I didn't want anybody to tell me how I can live or what I can do. And it's something that makes you lie. If you get a day's work and you make fifty dollars, you're not going to turn that day's work in. But it's a trap because when the youngest child turns eighteen, you don't have any retirement. You don't have any Social Security. You don't have anything. You're just an old person who raised all your kids on welfare."

This wise woman made so much sense. Here was her explanation of how crime got started among kids whose mothers are on welfare: "What you could buy for a two-year-old, you can't buy for a fifteen-year-old. So now, you're really in trouble because you've got a fifteen-year-old kid and you're still getting the same money that you started getting five years ago. So then, that's when you've got the tennis shoes that you can't afford and your kid wants to be like everybody and you can't afford to give it to him. And then he ends up on the streets." She talked about how "project women" raised "project kids." "Once you learn how to deal with the system, that little two-year-old or that little three-year-old is sitting there looking at you maneuver. And then she learns how to maneuver. And then it repeats itself over and over and over again. And I didn't want that for my children. My mother didn't give it to me, and I didn't want that for my children."

Eva Oliver knew she wanted out of "the system." As she says, that check that comes for free comes with too high a price. But she doesn't think that women on welfare can simply pull themselves up by the bootstraps, go out and find jobs, and become constructive members of society. It's not that simple. And as she concocted her prescription for the welfare mess, I wished I could pack her onto the plane with me and take her back to Washington to talk to the people writing the laws.

"I think the answer is it's better to help a person some and let him help himself some. And then, as he helps himself, then give him less until it balances out. In other words it's like raising a child. Once you have it, you have to keep nurturing it until it grows to stand on its two feet. So, just saying, 'In two years we're going to cut them off'—no. Because you created this system and kept them babies all this time. And now, all of a sudden, you're going to cut the cord? Uh-uh. That won't work."

What does work, according to Eva Oliver, is a good training program. Those programs have come in for a lot of criticism as an ineffective and costly use of taxpayer dollars. She herself had once been in a Job Corps program that didn't make her self-sufficient. What was it about this training that made the difference? "They gave us a lot of love. They made you believe in yourself. It was a hug, a pat on the hand. It was a time of healing. It was a time of learning. They taught you how to dress for an interview, how to talk, what to say, what not to say. And they gave you that extra pat on the back: 'Girl, you can do it. This is the greatest class that ever came through here.' And then they sent you out of the door, and you went out with your little bag swinging in your hand, 'I'm going to conquer the world.'" If the first job didn't come through, they'd send you to another, giving the sense all the time that they cared, that they believed. How simple. And how rare.

But, even with that kind of encouragement, Eva Oliver would not have made it, she's convinced, without her family. She had the values of hard work and perseverance passed down by her father and mother and grandmothers, and she had her sisters and brothers pitching in to take care of her kids when she worked the swing shift or stayed for overtime. "Everybody's not going to be in the same situation that I was in, that I had sisters and brothers so close around me. But then, you look through the community and you find somebody who can help you with your kids. And if you have to pay them, then pay them. Working gives you your pride and dignity back. And then you, in turn, pass that down to your kids and say, 'If you work hard, you can have all the good things in life, too. You don't have to take the shortcuts like stealing something out of a grocery store. If you work for something, you can walk in and demand somebody sell this to you.'"

It's a message she has conveyed not only to her own children but to many women on welfare. Eva Oliver believes deeply in "giving back." So when she could, she would pick up the rent and utility bills of other women in need. She even took some into her home. For a while there her phone number was "all over the place," as a resource for other women. She went to the training center to work with the women coming up through the program and found ways to improve it. And her company, Allied Signal, gave her time to go proselytize to other welfare mothers about the value of work. She always tempered her enthusiasm, however, with a warning—don't go for a blue-collar job unless you're ready for it. "Most women will come out and say, 'I don't have to do this.' So they'll walk away from it. If you're sure this is what you want to do, fine. For God's sake, go ahead. But if you're not sure, then don't mess it up for somebody else." It's tough, tough work at Allied Signal, Eva Oliver advised other women, made tougher for her because she didn't start until she was thirty years old and because she was the groundbreaker, the one who had to prove she could do it, and the one who had no one to turn to when the men gave her a hard time. Her age might have made her situation more difficult, but even younger women found the physical punishment brutal. For a long time, Eva Oliver just laughed off the beating her body was taking. "When my muscle wears out, my brain kicks in," she would joke.

And she kept learning new things—at one point adding welding school to her résumé: "I'll probably forever be in somebody's school doing something. And I think everybody should. If you want to be successful, then educate yourself. This is the key. We just browbeat this: 'You have to go to school, you have to go to school, you have to go to school.' If you work hard in school, then you can have the American dream. You can have the house, the family, the car, or whatever it is that you want to be." It's the oldest of messages from American parents to their children. But somewhere along the way it got lost in the welfare system. The connection somehow got severed. No one believed it was possible, that the old "Go to school, work hard, and you will succeed" adage applied to them. Eva Oliver has done her best to bring it back, both for her own kids and for the dozens of women she counseled and cared for. "It's just like you've got to help. You've got to give something back. I felt like I had gotten so much, and God has left me so much that I had to give something back." She was able to "give back" to one of the sisters who helped her when she was down, taking in her twelve-year-old niece when that sister was incapacitated by a stroke. And Louisiana governor Mike Foster was smart enough to call on Eva Oliver's experience by appointing her to the Governor's Workforce Development Commission, where she could educate the state on welfare-to-work proposals, making life better for the women who came after her.

I don't want to imply that there's been anything easy about all of this. Just the opposite. This woman has toughed it out through all kinds of hardships, and in the end the years of backbreaking work as a first-class mechanic have taken their toll. "I was a big black woman in good old boys' territory and I paid for it," she told me when I caught up with her. She's had several operations on her shoulder and one on her knees. Her son, Richard Oliver, bought her lovingly built house with the big garden; she can't get down on her knees to turn the dirt anymore. But she plants pots in her smaller house, and it is filled with flowers—and grand-children. "We were blessed, all the kids did real well," she says—and that's what she was after. "I have sacrificed for them to give them the best life." And, with the enormous toll it took on her, she has. Her daughter, Shawna Oliver Wilder, is a registered nurse; her son coaches a high school football team, has one master's degree, and is working on another. And the niece she took in? "She's grown and has a baby of her own and she's working and going to school." She succeeded. Eva Oliver did not raise "project kids." Despite now debilitating aches and pains, putting on those overalls and that hard hat every day was worth it: "My kids got a better future and I taught them that hard work does pay off. I'm still grateful and I thank God for it. I'm still doing all right. . . . I did what I had to do." And she will keep at it. "As long as I can get up and do, I'll keep going," says this determined woman, "and I am going to encourage other people to keep going." And she will.

SCIENTIST

■   ■   ■

YEARS AGO WHEN I WAS FIRST WORKING AT NPR, I WOULD do some freelancing for a radio program produced by the American Association for the Advancement of Science. One day I was interviewing science historian Margaret Rossiter, who has written several books about women scientists, and she told the story of Christine Ladd-Franklin, a renowned mathematician and logician at the beginning of the twentieth century. After graduating from Vassar, Christine Ladd, as she was then, received a fellowship to study at Johns Hopkins in 1878 and completed all of the requirements for a Ph.D. in 1882. Even so, the university refused to grant her the degree because she was a woman. It wasn't until forty-four years later, after Ladd-Franklin had become famous, that Johns Hopkins officially dubbed her a doctor of philosophy. During the radio interview, the guest for the next segment of the show sat in the control room listening. She was a young scientist. I don't remember what she was there to talk about, but I remember vividly her reaction to the story she had just heard: she didn't believe it. Her reaction completely startled me. Here sat this person, who relied on data for her work, being presented with a piece of information so foreign to her own experience that she simply could not take it in. Instead, she chose to reject it. I was so dumbfounded that I could barely make it through the interview with her. And, of course, I wanted to kill her.

How could she be so ignorant of, and so ungrateful to, the women who came before her? But then, with the exception of a few Nobel Prize winners here and there, most of us are probably unaware of the contributions women have made to science over the centuries and the incredible obstacles they faced. I didn't know that nineteenth-century female scientists had to ask their husbands to present their papers to scientific societies because they were excluded, or that twentieth-century women often conducted their research without pay because antinepotism rules prevented them from collecting salaries from the same institutions as their husbands. Those rules prevented Nobel Prize–winning physicist Maria Goeppert-Mayer from holding a paying faculty position for most of her career. I did know that as late as the 1980s women were banned from private clubs where important scientists met. But I didn't understand the implications of that exclusion. When women I knew started militating to join a posh Washington men's club, I thought they were crazy. The food was horrible and most of the members had long since lost a pulse, as far as I could tell. I expressed that opinion to a fellow Wellesley alum one day, and she then testily explained to me that many of the decisions about scientific funding took place within those hallowed walls. To make her case for cash, she needed to get inside. The club finally voted to accept a few women a year. I don't know what effect that's had on money for scientific research, but the food has definitely improved.

For most of human history, women were shut out of the scientific "club" altogether, and not all of the stories of the handful of women who did break through the barriers end happily. The history books tell us about the Egyptian Peneshet, who was director of physicians at the medical school in Heliopolis circa 1500 B.C., and Homer sang of the female physician Agamede. Something happened after Homeric times (probably around the twelfth century B.C.), because women were legally barred from practicing medicine in Athens by the fourth century, the so-called Golden Age. Defying the law, Agnodike disguised herself as a man to study to become a doctor. When she was discovered and brought to trial, the women of Athens threatened mass suicide if she was convicted—her crime was punishable by death. After hearing of Agnodike's abilities from her female followers, the judge changed the law. Hypatia, a scientist in Alexandria, Egypt, in the fourth century A.D., didn't fare as well. A mathematician and astronomer who wrote major works in both fields, Hypatia followed her father as director of the Museum of Alexandria, the equivalent of a large university. She was also a talented and prolific inventor, devising an instrument to remove salt from seawater, another to measure the level of water, plus a navigational instrument for determining the positions of the sun, stars, and planets. The Roman rulers of the city called on her for advice and counsel. But the bishop denounced her and all other prominent pagans as evil. Eventually a "Christian" mob seized Hypatia, dragged her into a church, and dismembered her with sharpened oyster shells.

With that charming story, the history of women in science goes dark for about fifteen hundred years. Occasional references can be found to exceptions here and there—in fifteenth-century Frankfurt, Jewish women served as doctors, for example. But in sixteenth-century England, women were outlawed as healers, and in seventeenth-century America, Margaret Jones was hanged as a witch for practicing herbal medicine and healing. (The Dutch colonists were more liberal; the first hospital in New Amsterdam was run by a woman.) Even so, women learned about science, went to scientific meetings, and even wrote popular books on scientific subjects. But in the nineteenth century, when the role of research in science grew, women's participation diminished, as people without official scientific degrees, amateurs who simply loved the study of science, were no longer welcome. In the United States, women and science were portrayed as antithetical. Science was rational, competitive, and impersonal; women were irrational, delicate, and emotional. The whole idea of a "female scientist" was considered unnatural. Still, some women managed, despite the odds, to invade the universities and laboratories, the hospitals and asylums. Midwives, nurses, and nuns were received with varying degrees of acceptance in the healing professions, but cracking the doctors' ranks was so difficult that the few women who did have become legendary. In 1835 Harriot and Sarah Hunt, sisters in Boston, opened a practice that emphasized hygiene, rest, and diet. Harriot decided she needed more formal training, so she applied to and was accepted by Harvard Medical School in 1850. But the male students protested so noisily when she showed up for lectures that she eventually withdrew from the hostile institution. In reaction, the Harvard trustees voted to exclude women from the medical school the following year, a ban that lasted until 1946. The first woman in America who was actually able to receive a medical degree was Elizabeth Blackwell, who pioneered in what was to become the hallmark of many women in medicine—ministering to poor women and children.

Raised by a progressive father who thought his girls should have the same education as his boys, Blackwell decided to study medicine in 1844 after she visited a dying friend who told her that she would have gotten medical care sooner if she could have seen a woman doctor. Blackwell discreetly asked some doctor friends about attending medical school, only to be answered with shocked outrage that she should even think of such a thing. She found a physician who would train her privately, but she needed a degree in order to practice. Sixteen medical schools turned her down before Geneva Medical College in upstate New York accepted her, thinking it was a joke. When the dean read her letter of application to his charges, they thought students at a nearby college were putting them on. Their tongue-in-cheek response—"In extending our unanimous invitation to Elizabeth Blackwell, we pledge ourselves that [she shall never] regret her attendance at this institution"—was taken at face value by the eager Elizabeth. When a flesh-and-blood female showed up to take classes, the surprised school stood by the dean's letter. The townspeople and wives of faculty members were less than pleased by this freak in their midst, going so far as to cross the street to avoid her, but she received her degree at the top of her class in 1849. A medical degree was one thing, a medical practice another. American hospitals wouldn't accept her for further training, so Blackwell went to Paris, where she was relegated to a midwifery course, and then on to London and to St. Bartholomew's teaching hospital.

Back in the United States, she tried to set up shop in New York City. In one boardinghouse where she rented a room for patient visits, all of the other boarders moved out when they learned there was a lady doctor in the house. The lectures she delivered to make ends meet attracted some liberal-minded Quaker women who became her first patients, providing her with a steady income. Finally, with some cash coming in, Blackwell was able to fulfill her dream of setting up a free clinic for poor women and children. Despite their misgivings about a female doctor, two hundred women with no other option for health care visited the part-time clinic in its first year of operation. In 1857 Elizabeth Blackwell with her younger sister, Emily, who had also become a doctor, and a third female physician, Marie Zakrzewska, who had recently arrived from Europe, opened the New York Infirmary for Indigent Women and Children. Liberal and reform groups from far and wide had helped finance this first hospital staffed entirely by women, but the neighbors were not so sure they approved. The first couple of deaths brought on attacks by angry mobs convinced the lady doctors were killing their patients. But the hospital survived; in fact an expanded version of it—the Strang Clinic—still operates at the same location on Fifteenth Street today.

After the Civil War, when the Blackwell sisters helped train nurses for the battlefield, the women fulfilled another dream. They established the Women's Medical College (which merged with Cornell Medical School in 1899) to ensure that female doctors received as rigorous an education as the men. In addition to its regular courses, the college sent students into the tenements of New York to teach hygiene and health care to poor people. Other doctors signed up to train under Dr. Blackwell, including Rebecca Cole, the second black woman, after Rebecca Lee Crumpler, to receive an M.D. By the time Elizabeth Blackwell died in 1901, she had started a movement; there were more than seven thousand women doctors in America, and many of them dedicated themselves to serving mothers and children of all races and classes.

The New York City Department of Health hired another gutsy woman, Dr. Sarah Josephine Baker, to experiment with her theories of preventive health care. In 1908 she recruited thirty nurses to go into the city's slums to explain the importance of cleanliness and promote breast-feeding for infants. In a clever bit of dealing with reality, Baker established Little Mothers' Leagues, hoping to help young girls care for their baby siblings while their mothers went to work. In ten years her efforts cut the city's infant mortality rate almost in half. Then another woman doctor, Alice Hamilton, went beyond the tenements into the workplace, where she raised issues about safety and health that resulted in first-of-its-kind legislation guaranteeing some basic workers' protections.

Alice's father lost his grocery wholesale business when she was a teenager, so she set about finding a job in which she could support herself and be of some use. The first state medical school to admit women, the University of Michigan, accepted her in 1892, granting her the M.D. a year later. When she started teaching and conducting research in Chicago, she provided the same kind of care for mothers and children at Hull House, the famous settlement house, that Sarah Baker was offering in New York. There Hamilton met working men and women who were seriously sick, and she began to suspect the cause might be the poisons they encountered on their jobs. The doctor's interest in industrial hazards came to the attention of the governor of Illinois, who put her in charge of a commission studying work-related illnesses. After a good deal of resistance from both companies and workers fearful for their jobs, in 1910 Hamilton published her report documenting extensive lead poisoning in factory workers. Illinois passed what was essentially the first workers' compensation law a year later—establishing safety and health standards and providing payments to people who got sick or injured on the job.

Considered one of the nation's experts on industrial health, Hamilton was commissioned by the U.S. Department of Commerce to conduct a national survey of all kinds of places of work—not only factories but quarries, mines, construction sites, mills—looking for all kinds of poisons. Eventually the work paid off, as state after state enacted laws similar to the one in Illinois. Hamilton's expertise paid off for her as well, up to a point. In 1919 Harvard gave her a position in the new Department of Industrial Medicine at the medical school as the university's first female faculty member. But she was never treated as a full-fledged colleague by the men—they refused to let her into the faculty club, told her she couldn't march in the commencement procession, and declared football tickets off-limits. Worse than that pettiness, the school kept her at the assistant professor level for the sixteen years she was at Harvard, even though she wrote two textbooks and was called on constantly by governments and businesses as a consultant on industrial medicine.

In 1959, forty years after Harvard timidly took on Alice Hamilton, the Johns Hopkins University School of Medicine appointed Helen Taussig as a full professor in pediatrics. (Hopkins had opened at the turn of the twentieth century with the help of donations by the "Ladies of Baltimore," who insisted that women be admitted on a par with men.) By that time Taussig was one of the best-known physicians in the country, having conceived of the operation that saved thousands of newborns with heart defects—so-called blue babies. Taussig was hailed as such a prominent professor of pediatrics that doctors came from around the world to study under her. That's how in 1962 she learned from a West German doctor about children being born in Europe with severe birth defects and the suspicion that they might be caused by a new drug called thalidomide. Taussig rushed off to Europe to investigate, returned home, and presented her findings to another female doctor, Frances Kelsey, who headed the new drug division at the Food and Drug Administration. Kelsey had already withstood enormous pressure from thalidomide's U.S.

manufacturer as she adamantly refused to allow the drug on the U.S. market, insisting that the company had not proved its safety. But until the two women swung into action, obstetricians in this country were handing out samples of the pill for "test" purposes. Taussig and Kelsey's warnings prevented thousands of American women from taking the drug and producing the severely damaged "thalidomide babies" seen all over Europe. It was one of the first times that the "old girls' network" exercised its embryonic clout on behalf of mothers and babies, but certainly not the last.

Birth defects also became the focus of Virginia Apgar's work. As an anesthesiologist, she had specialized in childbirth in the 1930s and 1940s—and became concerned that newborn babies were just wrapped up and shuttled off to the nursery without anyone examining them. She developed a series of simple tests to be given immediately after birth to tell whether a baby was in danger and needed immediate attention. Proud parents still brag about their newborns scoring a perfect 10 on the Apgar test. Later in life Apgar left Columbia's College of Physicians and Surgeons (where she had been named the first female full professor in 1949) to go back to school for a master's degree in public health. From there she went on to a position with the March of Dimes, where she worked to prevent birth defects for the rest of her life.

Whenever I hear about "the first woman to . . ." I know she's someone I'd like to meet, because her story is bound to be an interesting one. In the field of medicine, it's also because

I know she's likely to have used that newly integrated position to try to better the lot of women and children. It's no accident that it was the "first woman" to become the medical director of Cook County Hospital in Chicago, Rowine Brown Truitt, who successfully lobbied for a law requiring doctors to report suspected cases of child abuse. And it was the "first woman" surgeon general of the United States, Antonia Novello, who dedicated her tenure in the early 1990s to the health concerns of children and women. And it was the "first woman" to head the National Institutes of Health, Bernadine Healy, who enforced rules that women be included equally with men in scientific testing. So it's good news for women and children that the twenty-first century began with women making up half of the medical school population. (In 2006, 72 percent of actual practicing physicians were still male. But that's down from 92 percent in 1970!) It's a far cry from the day Elizabeth Blackwell was admitted as a joke to become the "first woman" to receive a medical degree in the United States.

As tough as life has been for women in medicine, it's been even tougher for their sisters in other sciences. Women dabbled in botany and geology and entomology in the early years of this country, some of them were probably serious scientists, but no one ever recognized them for their work.

One of the first fields where women made their mark was astronomy, where "amateurs" acting on their own could make scientific discoveries. Maria Mitchell was a librarian on the Massachusetts island of Nantucket on an October night in 1847 when she saw a strange object through the telescope she and her father had set up on top of the building where they lived. She knew it was a comet, but not one she had ever seen before in her years of stargazing. Her father reported the find to the head of the Harvard Observatory, and Maria received a gold medal from the king of Denmark, who had promised it to the next person to spot a new comet. With a celestial object now named after her (officially titled Comet Mitchell, 1847), Mitchell in 1848 became the first woman elected to the American Academy of Arts and Sciences, a position that allowed her into the great observatories of the world. After brewer Matthew Vassar established his women's college in Poughkeepsie, New York, in 1861, he asked Mitchell to head the observatory and teach astronomy four years later, making her the first female astronomy professor in the world. She also helped found the Association for the Advancement of Women, saying, "I believe in women even more than I do in astronomy." In addition to her comet, a crater of the moon is named after Maria Mitchell.

An even more remarkable story of an astronomer is that of Williamina Fleming, one of a group of women called "Pickering's harem," who worked under Edward Pickering at the Harvard Observatory. Fleming and her husband had immigrated to America from Scotland in 1878, but they had barely set foot on these shores when the husband deserted his pregnant wife. She found work as a maid at Pickering's house and, as the tale is told, one day when the professor was frustrated with one of his Harvard students he exploded, "My Scottish maid could do it better." So Pickering decided to see if he was right. He brought Fleming on to help him with his massive task of classifying each star according to its spectrum. She was eventually put in charge of the star survey, and in 1899 received the first appointment ever given to a woman by the Harvard Corporation. Her work on star classification plus some original discoveries earned her the first place for an American woman in the British Royal Astronomical Society.

One of the women who studied under Mina Fleming was Annie Jump Cannon, who eventually took over Fleming's job. As a little girl, Cannon showed such a fascination with the skies that her mother set up an observatory of sorts in the attic. The obviously intelligent young woman went off to the fledgling female college Wellesley for her undergraduate degree and later returned for a master's. She was allowed to use the Harvard Observatory as a special student in astronomy at Radcliffe, and there she became a member of the "harem." (Pickering had managed to hire all of those women by appealing to the Harvard Corporation's pocketbook. He explained that the women could do the job just as well as men for about one-third the salary.) At the observatory Cannon probably examined more stars—some 350,000 of them—than any other person on earth. She was awarded a gold medal by the National Academy of Sciences in 1931, a female first, but she wasn't offered membership. She was, however, named to an endowed chair at Harvard in 1938.

A long line of distinguished women astronomers started their careers in the Harvard Observatory, or can trace their education to the women who were there. When I was at Wellesley, there were some renowned astronomers on the faculty and a sophisticated observatory for so small a school. I thought the study of the stars involved some romantic peering into the heavens while ruminating on Greek philosophers. Imagine my dismay when it turned out to require trudging through the snow on wintry nights to the observatory to tackle hard science—much more physics than philosophy. I barely struggled through—with profound admiration for the women, and men for that matter, who excelled in the field.

Wellesley started offering astronomy in 1879, under the direction of Sarah Whiting, who had opened what was only the second undergraduate physics laboratory in America at Wellesley the year before. Whiting was one of several women in the Boston area trying to break through the scientific barriers. The most famous among them was chemist Ellen Swallow Richards, who is credited by many with founding the science of ecology. Ellen Swallow studied astronomy at Vassar under Maria Mitchell, but she majored in chemistry and then, in 1870, went as the first female to the newly opened Institute of Technology in Boston, what was to become MIT. Swallow wrote that she later learned that the school had waived her tuition fees not because of her need, but so that the president "could say I was not a student, should any of the trustees or students make a fuss about my presence." She insisted that she wouldn't have gone there "had I known on what basis I was taken." Though she completed the requirements for a Ph.D., the school would not award the degree to a woman. Even so, she was able to do important work at MIT, teaming up with one colleague to examine the water supply in Massachusetts for the state board of health. Another colleague, Robert Hallowell Richards, encouraged her interest in metals and mining—and in him. They were married in 1875, and Ellen Richards was inducted as the first female member of the American Institute of Mining and Metallurgical Engineers in 1879.

By then, Ellen Richards had helped establish a women's chemistry laboratory at MIT, where she worked, without pay at first, until the school integrated women into its regular program in 1883. Then she joined a new MIT lab studying "sanitary chemistry," in which scientists analyzed food, air, and water. Presciently, at the end of the nineteenth century Richards wrote, "The day is not far distant when a city will be held as responsible for the purity of the air in its school-houses, the cleanliness of the water in its reservoirs, and the reliability of the food sold in its markets as it now is for the condition of its streets and bridges." Not only did Richards continue her studies of water purity, but the state also asked the lab to take a look at grocery samples, in order to create food safety standards in the Massachusetts Food and Drug Act. As she became more and more convinced that the average housewife could help prevent illness and accidents, Richards developed the idea of scientific home management. Her theories became formalized in yet another new field called home economics. With some others who shared her interests, Richards founded the American Home Economics Association in 1908 and became its first president. It's easy to see how her emphasis on everyday household management plus her extensive knowledge of air, water, and food pollution would lead Richards to try to put them together. She proposed in 1892 a new science to be called "oekology," from the Greek word for "household." *Ecology* has come to mean the study of the household of the universe, but its beginnings and those of consumer science clearly owe a debt to Ellen Richards.

Building on the work of these nineteenth-century women, including my old friend Christine Ladd-Franklin, female scientists in the twentieth century moved slowly, oh so slowly, into the mainstream ranks. It was hard for the scientific establishment to ignore the likes of Hattie Elizabeth Alexander, who found a way to prevent most deaths caused by a form of meningitis, or Alice Evans, who discovered that unpasteurized milk caused disease, or Florence Sabin, who uncovered new and important information about the blood and immune systems. Then came World War II, and Uncle Sam needed female scientists. About eighty-five women worked on the Manhattan Project to develop the atom bomb, including Leona Woods Marshall, who helped design the first nuclear reactor. World War II also brought Grace Hopper into the navy, where she designed Flow-Matic, the computer language that gave birth to data processing.

During the war, the National Academy of Sciences admitted Barbara McClintock for her work in genetics. Despite that highly unusual recognition, McClintock felt she never received the support she needed or the promotions she thought she deserved in the academic world. She spent most of her working life in the laboratories at Cold Spring Harbor, New York, closely following the genes in corn, making the discovery that genes are not fixed but fluid. Along the way, her findings about "jumping" genes were at best ignored, at worst ridiculed, until decades later new research on DNA proved her right. Now considered one of the greatest geneticists of all time, McClintock won the Nobel Prize for her landmark work in 1983, almost forty years after her surprising discovery, the only American woman ever to win a Nobel Prize in the sciences that was not shared with a man.

Though the concept of "female scientist" might no longer be considered unnatural, as it was in the early nineteenth century, it's still not all that ordinary in the more prestigious sciences. In 2007, though more than two-thirds of the doctorates in psychology were awarded to women, and almost half of those in the social sciences, the numbers drop sharply to barely more than a quarter as you move into mathematics, chemistry, physics, and astronomy, and they drop even more—to 18 percent—in engineering and computer science.

In early 2009 one of those women with a computer science degree, Carol Bartz, was picked to head Yahoo, a Fortune 500 company. It makes you think that if more women held those degrees, they, too, could get plum jobs. But it's not just in the student ranks that the numbers are sparse. Female faculty members teaching science and engineering are even fewer and farther between. In 2003 the National Science Foundation concluded that women held 28 percent of the full-time university positions in those fields and made up only 18 percent of the full professors. Those numbers sparked a major academic controversy in 2005 when then Harvard University president Lawrence Summers, saying that he was trying to be provocative, set off a firestorm in giving what he thought could be the reasons for underrepresentation of women in the sciences. It might be, he mused, that there is a clash between "legitimate family desires and employers' current desire for high power and high intensity," or that "in the special case of science and engineering, there are issues of intrinsic aptitude." What he didn't seem to think was much of a problem were "lesser factors involving socialization and continuing discrimination." At least one woman scientist stood up and walked out of the speech—others went directly to the press. They couldn't believe what they were hearing. Girls had less "intrinsic aptitude" than boys when it came to science? The ways girls were directed in school and the way women were treated in the workplace were "lesser factors" when it came to the disproportionately low numbers of full-time female faculty members? This from the president of the country's most prestigious, for better or worse, university! A president who had offered only four out of thirty-two tenured positions to women in the previous school year! My daughter, who has covered science and technology for radio and TV and is something of a techno-nerd, went into full cry. "I can't believe," she correctly howled, "that we still have to put up with this stuff in the twenty-first century." We didn't give my mother, who had worked in Congress on programs to promote women in science, the opportunity to chant, *"Plus ça change . . ."*—we said it for her. It was all so disheartening.

But a few good things did come out of the whole debacle. Summers, trying to save his skin, appointed committees to find ways to recruit, retain, and promote women in the sciences at Harvard. The best way to recruit women was to get rid of him—and that was the next good thing that happened. Summers was forced out as Harvard president and a woman, Drew Gilpin Faust, was selected to replace him. And then, just in case Larry Summers thought this was all some tempest in a Harvard faculty teapot, when the newly elected president Obama started putting together his team, the former Treasury secretary was deemed unconfirmable. His job in the administration would have to be one that did not require Senate approval.

Women scientists can give you a lot of reasons why girls don't follow them into their fields—teachers and parents don't encourage girls the way they do boys; girls know that there's still a good deal of discrimination against women in science; the lack of women is self-perpetuating because there aren't enough role models. One woman in science is devoting her life to changing all of that—physicist and former astronaut Sally Ride. If there's one role model girls are likely to want to follow, Sally Ride is it. A girl who dropped out of college to play tennis (she was nationally seeded but realized she was better at science than on the court) and then went back to get a graduate degree in physics from Stanford, Sally Ride captured the attention of the country when she took off into space as the youngest and first American female astronaut in 1983. The just-turned-thirty-two-year-old successfully completed that mission aboard the *Challenger* space shuttle and went back up on the spacecraft the next year. It was while she was training for a third flight that the *Challenger* exploded in midair, and Ride was called to serve on the commission investigating the accident, a job she also performed after the space shuttle *Columbia* disintegrated.

When she left NASA, after overseeing the space agency's long-term strategic plan, Ride started teaching physics at the University of California in San Diego and writing books aimed at getting kids—especially girls—interested in science. And now she has created a company, Sally Ride Science, whose Web site declares that "a key part of our corporate mission is to make a difference in girls' lives, and in society's perceptions of their roles in technical fields." The company does that through festivals and special camps for elementary- and middle-school girls, and through books, games, and other resources for kids, teachers, and parents. In one question-and-answer session when she was asked what she thought about Larry Summers's remarks, Ride said her first reaction was "What was he thinking?" And she's armed with statistics showing that given a chance girls do as well as boys. She pointed to the fact that in fourth grade two-thirds of both girls and boys like science, but then girls lose interest at a higher rate than boys do. By the time they reach high school, five times as many boys as girls say they want to major in engineering. The disparity, she said flatly, "doesn't come from any innate biological difference" but from a culture and society that make "girls think science and engineering is not for them, and of course we know that's not the case."

Sally Ride is doing her best to make sure it's not the case. And other women astronauts who have come after her— scientists all—are providing visible role models for girls who may look at them and decide that science is "cool," to use Sally Ride's word. She knows that girls still worry that boys won't like them if they star in something as brainy as physics or engineering. Brawny girls have become popular— but although the old "boys don't make passes at girls who wear glasses" rap might not be uttered out loud anymore, too many girls still believe it's true.

W I F E

◼   ◼   ◼

WHEN STEVE AND I GOT MARRIED IN 1966, ONE OF THE
most useful wedding presents we received was *Webster's Third
New International Dictionary,* unabridged. In the pre-Internet
era, the hefty tome served us well as it traveled around the
world with us. One day out of curiosity I looked up the
word *wife*. First definition? "Woman." That pretty much
sums up the attitude of 1966: to be a woman was to be a
wife. The dictionary goes on to list other meanings under
the primary definition: "a woman acting in a specified ca-
pacity . . . one who sells something . . . (a fishwife) . . . one
who has charge of something . . . (henwife) . . . a woman
worker (washerwife)." Never does that most-used term
"housewife" appear. I suppose it was considered tautological

at the time. Not until the second definition do we get "a married woman."

Why am I surprised? After all, the celebrant at the marriage ceremony itself declared us "man and wife." Isn't that saying the same thing, to be a woman is to be a wife? I certainly thought so. Even the nuns who taught me, for whom I had great affection and respect, called themselves "brides to Christ." My goal in life was marriage, then motherhood. I wanted to get married as soon as possible after college, do something interesting for a while, but have babies as fast as I could. Then I thought I would stay home, do good things in the community, and enhance my husband's career. That's what suburban life in the 1950s seemed to dictate, and I believed then and believe now that it's a worthy way to spend a life. It's what my friends' mothers did, although, interestingly, not what my own mother did. It's what any man I could expect to marry would certainly expect.

Steven and I never had that conversation; we never even thought about it. When we met, in the summer of 1962, at the ages of eighteen and nineteen, the subject wasn't on the table. It's about the only one that wasn't—since we were at a student political convention in Columbus, Ohio. Debates raged fiercely over racism and imperialism and capitalism; no one had heard of sexism. When we went back to school and eventually started dating, nothing mattered but young love. As we started to "get serious," only two topics disturbed our reverie: how could we reconcile our religious differences, and when would he bite the bullet and marry me? Debating the religion question—he's Jewish, I'm Catholic—served to concentrate our minds on how we felt about family and how we envisioned our lives unfolding. Those late-adolescent agonies at times seemed unfixable. But a lot of tearful conversations and a little growing up helped us come to an agreement about how we would handle religion; then it was just a question of getting Steven to pop the question. After all, I was twenty-two years old, watching "the best years of my life" swirl down the drain. Finally, after I threatened to "go to California," which sounded to me like a realistic version of Timbuktu, he proposed. The setting, or more to the point, the setup, was a carriage ride in Central Park. We were almost out of the park by the time he finally said the magic words, not that I'm still holding that against him after all these years. As to the religion part, the solution in retrospect seems simple. And the process of coming to it shaped the way we handled many future difficulties. We chose the path of inclusion, not exclusion. We practice both religions. We were married in an ecumenical ceremony in the garden of the home I hold so dear. The children were raised in both religious traditions, learning more about religion than many kids of their era, and celebrating Christian and Jewish holidays. It can get a little expensive and more than a little exhausting at certain seasons but it's worked. In all our married years not one argument has been over religion. I can't say the same about work. We've had many a "heated discussion," as the politicians say, over the appropriate allocation of each other's time between work and family.

Not only did the rules change on the state of modern American matrimony just as we were entering into it, our own expectations, especially my own expectations, changed as well. But never comfortably. Most domestic debates dealing with my role as wife have stemmed from my own ambivalence and overriding guilt, feeling that wherever I was I should have been someplace else. When we got married, we never even talked about my job situation. Even though I loved anchoring a TV show and it was a great opportunity for such a young woman, we both took it for granted that I would quit and move to New York with Steven, and so did everyone else, including my own mother, who has always worked. I assumed that having achieved my goal, having been awarded the title "wife," I would settle into a bower of bliss.

What we settled into instead was a rent-controlled apartment on the West Side near what was then "Needle Park." When we arrived there after our honeymoon, a sign in the elevator read "No heat or hot water until further notice." And if Steven had tried to carry me across the threshold, he would have had a rough time because the previous tenants had taken up the floor in a fit of New York nastiness. I did love playing house—furnishing the apartment, making things pretty, cooking grown-up meals in our miserable little kitchen. But my efforts to create "home sweet home" were thwarted by my cash flow. Until I went to work, we had to stretch Steve's salary to cover two. As my attempts to find a job strung out for weeks, then months, we decided we better put a halt to most purchases. Because I hated asking my parents for money, I had always baby-sat or found odd jobs even as a kid. Now as an adult I felt like I was asking my husband for money. Even though we had a joint checking account, and even though Steven has never been anything but incredibly generous, it made me miserable that all the deposits were his.

It got pretty depressing—getting all dressed up to go sell myself in yet another interview, only to get turned down, and it reached the point where I was ready to do just about anything. But the days without one of those dreaded appointments could be even worse. When winter came on, I discovered that the building superintendent turned off the heat during the day with the clear message that no one should be home. It was cold and it was lonely. I couldn't wait for the day to be over so I could see Steven. Poor boy, loving me wasn't enough; he was supposed to entertain me as well. In doing some research on marriage, I've discovered that I was simply following in my foremothers' footsteps. In eighteenth-century America, female friends and relatives would help a woman adjust to her new situation, often staying with the young couple for the first months of marriage, making sure the bride met other women, even accompanying the newly-weds on their wedding trips. Can you imagine anyone trying that in this day and age? By the early nineteenth century, writers were describing "marriage trauma," where women sank into depression at the prospect of becoming someone's mate. They seemed to understand better than my generation did what it would mean to lose independence. Letters and diaries from the period make these women sound downright desperate. One wrote to her fiancé, "Every joy in anticipation depends on you, and from you must I derive every pleasure." In the latter part of the century, as women became educated, many opted out of marriage altogether. According to historian Sara Evans, nearly half of all college-educated women in the late nineteenth century never married.

Maybe it would have made a difference if I had known any of that when I was a newlywed. I doubt that I would have believed it. Now that I look back on that time, I realize what useful, if painful, lessons it provided. I learned that I need the company of other women. I learned that I perform much better with the discipline of a schedule. And I learned that I derive tremendous satisfaction from my work. I'm not particularly proud of those realizations. I think a more creative and self-contained person would do better on her own. But I'm awfully glad I found out about myself when I did. Fortunately, I had known Steven so long and loved him so much that I didn't even entertain the thought that marriage might be a mistake. Suppose I had not had that experience then, had not found out that I need work in order to be fulfilled? I probably would have discovered it after my first baby was born, and then I would have been truly tied up in knots about whether I was a failure as a mother.

When I finally did get a job at a small business newsletter in New York, I became a much happier human being. Steve probably became a much happier person as well, but he was nice enough not to tell me I had been driving him crazy. Still, there was no doubt that my work was secondary, something for me to do, not something that would merit any consideration in family decision making. My sweet husband still blushes when I remind him of a story from that time. He was extolling the virtues of living on the West Side of Manhattan, only one express subway stop from Times Square. "Now," he mused, "if I worked in the building where *Esquire* magazine is, for instance, then it would probably make sense to live on the East Side." In randomly picking a building as an example, he had unthinkingly chosen the exact place where I worked. It was one of those sensitive male moments. And, yes, getting to my job was a pain in the neck.

It clearly was taking some getting used to, this idea that we were two, not one, and that we had responsibility for each other. Early one morning the phone rang and the operator asked if we knew anyone in Oberlin, Ohio, who might have called us; they were having trouble identifying the calling number for billing purposes. I said no and hung up. Steven groggily asked who had called, I told him, and he protested, "But we do know someone in Oberlin. My brother goes to school there." "Yes," I responded, "but if the phone company can't figure out its billing, that's its problem." After I went to work I called Steve as a joke, disguised my voice, and said, "Mr. Roberts, did you lie to our operator this morning?" "No," he gulped, "that was my wife, C-O-K. . . ." As I burst out laughing, he knew he'd been caught.

The newsletter where I was working folded and I landed at a local television station in a job I didn't like very much. By the time I caught on that it wasn't the place for me, I was pregnant, much to my delight. I stayed until the baby was born, then quit. No such thing as maternity leave existed. The day we brought Lee home from the hospital, past the piles of garbage on the streets uncollected because of the sanitation workers' strike and the gaggles of schoolkids out on the streets because of the teachers' strike, the *New York Times* assigned Steven to Los Angeles. Neither of us had ever been there, but to me it had all the earmarks of a great adventure. Off into the sunset with my handsome husband and precious baby. The old Ford Falcon that carried us across the country didn't exactly have the look of a shining chariot, but we did land on a Malibu mountaintop over-looking the Pacific Ocean. Farewell, Needle Park; hello, Lotus Land.

Hibiscus and bougainvillea replaced the garbage-strewn streets and we settled into a romantic idyll. Except there were diapers and bottles. And Steve was away a lot of the time. In those days, the roles could not have been more clear. Steven's work came first. He would do what he could to accommodate me and the baby, but within the parameters of the job. Fortunately, my old boss Sophie Altman had just sold *It's Academic* to the local NBC affiliate. It worked out perfectly for everyone to have me produce the show out there rather than fly someone out from Washington all the time. It gave me something to do, someplace to go, some people to meet, and some checks to cash. That was the way both of us saw it. Most of the tapings were on weekends, when Steven often baby-sat. Otherwise, it was catch as catch can with child care, just as it is for most people still. Lots of friends and family came to visit, so I didn't feel lonely. I think some motherhood hormones must have kicked in as well because I was happy as could be. We even managed from time to time to sneak off on what I called have-an-affair-with-your-wife weekends.

When Lee was not quite two years old, Rebecca arrived. Life grew geometrically more complicated, as I had also taken on a research project on the youth vote for the Twentieth Century Fund. In those years, Steve and I also worked on magazine pieces together where I did most of the research and reporting, he did most of the writing. (I later found out that my mother was quite horrified by one we wrote for the *New York Times Magazine* on venereal disease. How did I know about all those awful things?) Steve became a sort of one-man journalism school for me, generously sharing a byline. Now we do that all the time, writing a weekly syndicated column together, but then it was key to my building a body of work. And we were both slowly becoming aware that someday that would make a difference.

We were not, after all, impervious to the world around us. Quite the contrary—we were reporting on it. That world, particularly in California in the early 1970s, resounded with the chants of revolution—the student movement, the antiwar movement, the black power movement, and the women's movement. Women who were my contemporaries were rising up, declaring their independence from many of society's strictures and institutions, including marriage. Women like me were beginning to voice complaints about our unequal roles, to stir up family arguments on the subject. Men like Steven were defensive on the one hand, trying to adapt on the other, taking on more child care when it was convenient, even washing a dish or two. While we were making minuscule adjustments, the world was turning topsy-turvy. I remember calling a prominent feminist who was a friend of Steve's for an article we were doing. I wanted to let her know I was married to him, but I was actually afraid to use the word *wife*. She would certainly, in my view, find it a disparaging term. I carefully formulated my sentence to say, "Steve Roberts is my husband." How much times had changed in the not very many years since acquiring the title "wife" had been my life's ambition.

Even with those changing times and our recently raised consciousness, not a lot changed in our own lives. When Rebecca was a few days old we were evacuated from our home because of big brush fires. Steve deposited me and the two babies and, fortunately, my mother in a downtown hotel and went out to cover the fires. I had an *It's Academic* taping scheduled that couldn't be canceled. (I had planned the date thinking the baby would not yet have arrived. How was I to know she'd be early?) So, I left the ten-day-old and the two-year-old with my mother in a hotel room and went to work. Mamma said, "When I had a ten-day-old, I was still in the hospital." I, oh so thoughtfully, shot back, "Take her to the hospital if you want. I have to go to work." That's the way it was. If you worked, you accommodated. There was never any question of the workplace or the family accommodating you. Luckily, I found jobs with schedules that were by and large flexible, and a baby-sitting family of girls that was by and large available. But no matter what I did, it was clear that my main employment was that of wife. Even people in my work world saw it that way. When a children's TV program I was producing was nominated for an Emmy, I received a certificate inscribed with my name. Instead of the name that appeared on the show's credits, "Cokie Roberts," the certificate reads "Mrs. Stephen [*sic*] Roberts." That, I think, says it all.

Even so, I was enough of a "working wife" that the editors of the *New York Times* were worried about it when they transferred Steven to Greece. Would I raise a ruckus the way some women suddenly were? They didn't want a harridan on their hands, and neither did Steven. But they were safe; it was another adventure as far as I was concerned. The newspaper helped by paying for me to travel with Steve some of the time, which made an enormous difference in my enjoyment of the years abroad. We always have such a good time together, working and laughing and loving our way through all kinds of silly situations. One night way in the east of Turkey we checked in at some godforsaken hotel where no woman had ever stayed. There were no private rooms, just dormitories. The innkeepers put all the other travelers in one dorm and left the other to Steve and me. The only heat came from a coal-burning stove that we were totally incapable of stoking into life. So we took all the blankets from every other bed and huddled together on one narrow mattress. When we woke up we were covered with soot, but we were still having a wonderful time.

In those years I found out something new about this wife business—or maybe more accurately, the husband side of that coin. With Steven away so much, I was forced to deal with the inconveniences of living in a foreign country, all on my own. And Greece was in transition—hired help didn't come cheap and time-saving devices didn't exist. I remember one day struggling to cut up a whole chicken, fantasizing about packages of chicken parts. Pretty pathetic. Most of the other American wives there had the backing of some major institution, like the U.S. government or big corporate offices, when they ran into the inevitable culture clashes.

One memorable old world–new reality dustup came

when I went to register the family as aliens. We started with Steven's documents, and the bureaucrats asked a series of questions, including, "Religion?" I told them, "Jewish," and they had no problem with that. When we got to my religion, they assumed it would be the same, and were highly confused when I said, "Catholic." They approached the line on the children's forms with some trepidation. What, they asked dubiously, were they? When I replied, "Both," they went nuts. "Impossible," they cried as they disappeared into a back room to thrash it out. I could hear the screams. "The father takes precedence," shouted one. "But he's not Christian," bellowed another. What a terrible choice I had presented them, between patriarchy and Christianity. Much to my amazement, Christianity won out.

By having to do everything myself I found out that I was actually a highly competent human being, which was gratifying. I didn't *need* Steven around, I *wanted* him around. Life was a lot more fun with him than without him. He also provided the anchor for our little brood. Early on, he decreed that Sundays would be family days; no one could accept any invitations or make any commitments. Sometimes we all chafed under that, but it turned out over the decades to be an essential part of our lives together, whether we were picnicking or playing games or pondering the fate of the universe. Emotionally, I had not even the slightest desire to manage on my own, but practically I could do it. That was a revelation. (I did think it was a little much, though, one day when Steve and the landlord sat in the living room drinking brandy while I was in the basement fixing the furnace.) It was also a revelation that I could report on my own. CBS News regularly ran my radio spots, and sometimes TV as well. Several magazines printed my articles. And Steve and I still wrote pieces together, so I kept my name in circulation, which helped considerably when I came back to Washington to start the dreaded job hunt.

Steven says now that the day my role shifted was the day I went to work at NPR. I would mark it a few weeks earlier than that—somewhere in the period after we got back to Washington and I realized necessity dictated that I have a full-time, well-paying job. Psychically, I had expected that. I knew Washington was a tough town, where a woman better have an answer to the "What do you do?" question or face ostracism. I hate that, and I think it's ridiculous. But I knew I didn't have the self-confidence to withstand it. What I had not expected was the money crunch. When we were married eleven years earlier, families could easily live on a *New York Times* reporter's salary in our neighborhood or one nearby. By 1977 that was impossible. So, work for me was no longer just a question of my personal satisfaction, where earning "pin money" would do. Now it was real, just like Steve's work.

Soon it was really just like Steve's work. We were covering the same beat, Capitol Hill, and we commuted together, often ate lunch together, and saw each other throughout the day in media mobs. Most of our colleagues knew we were married, of course, but one newcomer whispered to a friend, "Steve Roberts is having an affair with that reporter from National Public Radio." His news organization was more prestigious than mine at the time, and he made more money than I did, but there couldn't be any pretense that his work was more demanding than mine. Neither one of us could say, "You just don't understand, dear." And Steven couldn't walk in the door at the end of the day and plead for mercy from the worries of household and family. We walked in the door together.

Steven realized just how much our situations had changed when the *New York Times* asked him to go to Three Mile Island, to cover the accident at the nuclear plant. Normally, he would have just gotten in the car and gone, but I was already there, and the kids were nervous about it. He told the *Times* he couldn't do it to the kids; it would totally freak them to have two parents in what they saw as danger. Still, even as Steven was accepting my new role, he would often play on my always-at-the-ready guilt about working too hard. When I was covering Pope John Paul II's first visit to this country in 1979, one day I called home to hear Steven tell me that Becca had taken a fall at a friend's house and the friend's mother thought she might need stitches near her eye. As he was starting to do a whole guilt number on me, I interrupted him. "Save the guilt for later, Steven, and just listen to two words: *plastic surgeon*." He hung up, grumpy, but he did go right home and get her to the doctor.

Still, household and family fell mainly under my domain. Rosie, a Scottish woman who had taken care of the children in Greece, eventually came to live with us here and made life livable. But, as wife, it was still my responsibility to see to it that the children were in good shape physically and mentally, the house was reasonably well kept, food was in the refrigerator, and bills were paid. Steve, more and more, offered to help. I kept saying that helping wasn't the point—doing what I asked—it was doing it without my asking, taking responsibility, that's what I claimed to be after. In truth, though, I think I was always reluctant to give up the household reins. *Power* might be too strong a word, but maybe not. I wanted the house done the way I wanted it done. I wanted fresh flowers in the vases, even if it meant staying up until two in the morning to arrange them. I wanted good meals on the table and I enjoyed cooking them. I wanted big holiday celebrations and I was determined, no matter how hard I was working, to provide them. It was part of my definition of myself, my role as wife, a role I had no intention of abandoning. Steven didn't ask those things of me. There were times when he would have been a lot happier if I had kept it simpler. And there were times when he would have been a lot happier if I had paid more attention to his needs and wants, not exhausted all my energies on the children and the job and the household. What about him? Once, he told me that he felt like he was another item on my list of things to do. Ouch, that struck home. What kind of a wife was that?

A busy one, that's what kind. As I got busier and older I realized that wasn't the kind of wife I wanted to be for the years left to me. I wanted to have some time with my husband while we could still enjoy it. After all, we had experienced the disadvantages of having children in our early twenties when we had no money and no help. Now we could enjoy the advantages of that—the fact that we were still young when we became empty nesters, and that the "kids" were out and on their own while we still had some earning power. I realized that it was nuts at this stage of life to be showing up at work every Sunday, never having a weekend off. That became even truer once the grandchildren started arriving. Some of Steve's and my most joyful times together are the times we share with those precious children of our children. To miss that time because of a job didn't make sense to me. It's funny. Even though I met Steven when he was nineteen years old and saw himself as some sort of swashbuckling journalist, I always knew he would be a wonderful grandfather. Even when I was eighteen and starry-eyed, I had a mental image of him as a gray-haired granddad playing with little kids. (Good thing I didn't tell him that.

He would have *never* proposed.) And it turns out that I was right. He loves his title as "Teebs," and when I see him surrounded by little people listening intently to a story he's reading, my heart does a familiar little skip. What I didn't know as that young girl so long ago was what a kind and caring son to his elderly mother, and to his mother-in-law, Steve would become. Since his mother moved to Washington a few years ago, he has lovingly entertained and encouraged her. When I see her face brighten as he talks to her about her great-grandchildren, my devotion knows no bounds.

Still, change is never easy, particularly the fundamental change in roles that occurred in our marriage. After all, it went from me being the good *New York Times* wife to me being a fairly visible person because of my own accomplishments. When strangers started to recognize me, it was always uncomfortable for me if my husband was with me. And even at this stage there can be some dicey moments. Though Steven completely supports the work I do for nonprofits and understands why I do it, it does take me away from home on enterprises that aren't exactly family related. But as this odd institution called marriage continues to evolve, we find ourselves blessed by how much we love each other. Someone once told me that young people were duped by Romeo and Juliet, that what they shared was rare, that most people never come close to a romance like that. Well, lucky us. We're in the rare category. *Household Magazine* in

1870 published a fable about an oak and a vine. The man, of course, is the oak, the woman the vine. And the point, obviously, is that the vine can't grow independently of the oak. It's a subversive tale, designed to subjugate women. But there's a lot of truth in it for me. I could not have had the life I have had professionally had I not taken as my first job that of wife. I would never have had the confidence to do what I do without Steven's sustaining hand. And none of it would be worth anything without him.

ENTERPRISER

THE MORE I LEARN ABOUT EARLY AMERICAN WOMEN THE
more impressed with them I am. Whether it's the women of
Revolutionary times keeping body and soul together on the
home front while the men were off for years at a time, or
the women who traveled west to carve civilization out of
the wilderness, I have come to admire their incredible fortitude regardless of their fates. Not only were they managing
to make life possible for their own friends and families
while facing what would be for us modern women daunting
hardships, they also toiled to improve the lives of those less
fortunate than themselves. Despite legal and political hurdles, they managed to clothe, house, feed, and educate those

who were in need, and started a tradition thankfully carried forward by American women today.

As early as 1727 the Ursuline nuns started a school and hospital in what was then French New Orleans. They added an orphanage a couple of years later, and flouted custom by teaching children of all races and social stations. In New York it was a Protestant, Isabella Graham, who used the money from her posh school for girls to help establish the Society for the Relief of Poor Widows with Small Children; and in Philadelphia, it was a Jewish woman, Rebecca Gratz, who worked with other society women to establish first nonsectarian, which in that day meant Protestant, and then Jewish benevolent societies, orphanages, and schools. Fortunately, most of those early organizations kept records, so we can see just how political these women had to be as they went about the business of fashioning a social safety net.

Remember, married women could not own property. So these women couldn't buy the land for their orphanages in their own names—first they would have to incorporate, and the corporation could then hold title to the property. So, they would troop to the state legislature or whatever body had the power to authorize corporations (in Washington it was the Congress) and lobby for their cause. Then the women would have to go back to the legislature, as well as to the public, to seek funds, performing the still difficult task of persuading people to help the poor. Then they had to hire staff and manage the institutions. These clever women always made sure that the "treasuress," as they called the woman charged with keeping the books, was an "unmarried lady." Otherwise some married woman's husband might try to seize the assets of the corporation.

Among the enterprising women in this period, one of my personal favorites is Elizabeth Ann Seton, probably because I have such respect for the nuns who taught me. She's actually Saint Elizabeth, officially canonized by the Catholic Church in 1975, the first native-born American to achieve sainthood. I bet a lot of the people who dealt with her didn't consider her a saint. She accomplished so much; she had to step on a few toes along the way. Mother Seton's biographies always include a line that I just love; it goes something like "she is credited with founding the American parochial school system." That's one of those statements where my reaction is, "Excuse me? Could I hear a little more, please? That's totally extraordinary." And, of course, her story is. Born in New York shortly before the Revolution, she went from riches to rags. Her father was a noted doctor and she was a well-educated young woman, someone raised to show concern for the poor, which she did by working with Isabella Graham and Eliza Hamilton (wife of Alexander) on their benevolent work. She married a wealthy New York merchant, William Seton, and proceeded to have five children before he lost first his fortune, then his health. On what was supposed to be a restorative trip to Italy in 1803, Seton died, and the Anglican Elizabeth was consoled by

Italian Catholic friends. After she returned to New York Mrs. Seton converted to Catholicism, much to the horror of her family. The family cut her off, leaving her and the five children destitute.

In 1808 a priest in the Catholic state of Maryland asked her to move to Baltimore to start a school for girls, which she did with the help of several other women, including, despite the protests of the Seton family, two of her husband's sisters. Later that year, five children notwithstanding, Seton founded a religious order, the Sisters of Charity of Saint Joseph's, the first one to originate in this country. The women moved out to donated land in Emmitsburg, Maryland, to set up a mother-house for the order and there founded a free school for the indigent girls of the parish. It was the first parochial school in America. By the time she died, in 1821, Mother Seton had dispatched nuns to twenty communities across the nation, starting schools, opening orphanages, building hospitals. Think of what it must have been like for those women, setting out on their own in early America, battling anti-Catholicism in order to educate children and take care of the poor and sick. Nothing easy about any of it.

Clara Barton is another one whose story intrigues me. There's an old amusement park not far from my house where we used to hang out as teenagers. Recently the antique carousel and a children's theater have been refurbished and we bring our grandkids there from time to time. Next door is

Clara Barton House, run by the National Park Service. I always meant to learn more about this neighbor of mine. Finally, when the local Red Cross chapter asked me to present some awards to its star volunteers, I did. One of those intrepid Massachusetts women, Clara Barton established a free school in New Jersey, which grew from six to six hundred students in one year. When the school hired a male principal, she quit and moved to Washington where she worked in the Patent Office. With the arrival of a new administration, she lost her patronage and her job. Without work, Barton became "sickly," a pattern that repeated itself throughout her life. She went back to work in 1860, but then the Civil War broke out, allowing her to follow what was clearly her calling as the "Angel of the Battlefield." The night before the horrific battle of Antietam she wrote, "I was faint but could not eat; weary, but could not sleep; depressed, but could not weep." Her fears were more than justified—almost twenty-one thousand soldiers lay dead or wounded the next day. Clara Barton constantly drove mule wagons through fire, crossed battle lines, and, most remarkably, cut red tape to nurse sick soldiers and distribute supplies to them. She badgered President Lincoln into setting up a bureau of records to identify the missing and the dead. In the summer of 1865 at Andersonville she oversaw the marking of thirteen thousand graves with headstones. As someone whose father disappeared in an airplane that was never found, I have always had tremendous empathy for families of the missing in action. Clara Barton was the first to recognize the need for some certainty about death.

With war's end, she became "sickly" again (clearly depressed due to inaction) and headed for Europe to rest. That was a joke; she soon learned about the International Red Cross and was back in battle, this time in the Franco-Prussian War, where she made her way to the front. The Red Cross became her life. On her return to the United States, she established the American chapter. There's another one of those historical statements that boggles the mind. Congress in the late 1800s feared nothing more than "foreign entanglements." So it took tireless lobbying to finally convince the Senate to ratify the Geneva Convention, which formed the American Red Cross, in 1882. Even more remarkable, Barton got the whole organization to go along with what was called the "American amendment," which she authored. It mandated the Red Cross to provide relief for victims of natural disasters as well as war, an exponential increase in its duties. What politics must have been involved in that little coup! And what a life it then meant for Barton, who was off to the Ohio floods in 1884, provided relief to victims of Russian and Armenian famines in the 1890s, and at the age of seventy-seven went to Cuba for the Spanish-American War, where she was back on the battlefield. She set a pattern for all future wars, where Red Cross nurses have brought care and comfort by the tens of thousands. Barton herself was not much of an organization woman, and she was forced to step down as president of the Red Cross in 1904. But she continued her relief work for the next eight years until she died at her home in Glen Echo, Maryland, at the age of ninety.

Women have been willing to give of their time and talents for others throughout our history. Now we give of our "treasure" as well. For the first time, in 2005, women donated more money to charitable causes than men did—$21.7 billion compared with $16.8 billion. It used to be almost impossible to get women to give money because they didn't see it as their own—it was their husband's money or the family's money. But that's changed. A major life insurance company estimates that by 2010 women will control 60 percent of the country's wealth, and women now think they can give that money away if they want to. Not only do women give more money than men, they give it differently from men, according to the experts in women's philanthropy. Women aren't particularly interested in getting individual credit for their gifts. Rather, in city after city around the country (they numbered four hundred in 2007), they are joining together in "women's giving circles." There they pool their resources in order to make a major impact and then determine collectively where the money will go. "Women are looking for relevance, not tax deductions. They want to serve in some way. They feel it's their obligation and responsibility," writer and publisher Pamela Fiori told U.S. News. "[T]here's a lot more than baking cookies and making pies—all of which is well and good, but there's also a world out there that we can serve and make changes to." Making changes is what women are interested in, and some will go to extraordinary lengths to do it.

One, who was profiled by my daughter-in-law, Liza Roberts, in *Metro Magazine,* is Frances Alexander. When she moved from her home in Los Angeles to be near her daughter in Durham, North Carolina, the retired schoolteacher thought she would be taking a well-deserved rest and spending time with her grandchildren. But, as she told Liza, she had to do something when she picked up the newspaper and read about the huge numbers of high school dropouts in the community and their dangerous gang activities. She knew about a program in L.A. that had succeeded in bringing gang members back to school and decided—all on her own—to try to replicate it in Durham. How? She didn't know, but she knew she had to do something: "If I didn't feel like I was ordained to be doing this, I wouldn't be doing it. It takes up every single bit of strength that I've got."

It takes up every single bit of strength because it's such incredibly hard work to take on a troubled teenage kid. But she's doing it. With no funds from the city or county except a small grant from the Juvenile Crime Prevention Council, Alexander rented space and called on Duke University and a local private school for help with computers, furniture, and teachers. And she started saving teenagers.

She talked to Liza sixteen months after she opened her

school, called EDGE, an acronym for "Education, Development, Growth and Employment." By then the sixty-nine-year-old "retiree" had been so successful that the juvenile courts were sentencing kids to her school and the local high schools were sending troubled youngsters in her direction. Thirty kids had already earned high school equivalency diplomas and gone on to college or vocational school. And, Liza learned, these kids from violent, chaotic lives who would have most likely ended up behind bars, or under the earth, once they get to college they do fine: "I've found all of the EDGE kids more than ready for college," a local college administrator told her about the students who graduated from Alexander's program. "These kids have been dealt a bad hand in life, but they stand shoulder to shoulder with kids that have come from any other high school. I don't know how she does it." But Frances Alexander knows how. It's a question of not treating the kids "as something that needs to be fixed," as she summed it up for Liza. "We treat them with respect, with kindness. But if they break the rules, they're out." And there's always another kid on the waiting list ready to take the spot. Money is a constant challenge, despite the school's success, and despite the fact that jail would cost a whole lot more, but Frances Alexander remains stalwart in her conviction—now proven—that she can turn these kids' lives around, and she will do everything she can to make that happen.

Hers is an extraordinary story, but there are women like

Frances Alexander all over the country, doing whatever they can to make life better for others, as women have been doing since the country began. Though the EDGE school with its emphasis on gang members is going to enroll more boys, much of women's philanthropy and volunteer work is focused on girls. The data on the effects of girls' education both here and around the world is now accepted by all financial and development organizations, from the World Bank to Save the Children. Keep a girl in school, they all agree, and you increase the country's per capita income, decrease the birth rate, improve health care, and even contribute to greater transparency in government. Women in America, Abigail Adams chief among them, started militating for girls' education before this was even a country, and a series of young ladies' academies were opened after the Revolution, including the one in New York run by Isabella Graham and attended by Nelly Custis, Martha Washington's granddaughter, when George was president. Through the centuries since then, women like Emma Willard worked to establish better girls' schools with rigorous curricula and to train teachers for them. Then, through the mid- to late nineteenth century, fine women's colleges were established, sometimes as coordinate or "sister schools" to male institutions. By the mid-twentieth century the feisty females of the 1960s and '70s pushed their way into those male institutions, turning them into coeducational schools. Now, with national undergraduate enrollment close to 60 percent female,

I find it more than a little ironic that college admissions officers are scratching their heads, trying to find ways to attract men. This gender disparity is considered a crisis. No one seems similarly concerned that not even one-quarter of the full professors teaching these students is female. And I sure don't remember any sense of alarm when the undergraduate numbers were the other way around.

When I was in college the eight schools of the Ivy League were still male bastions, places you went to as a "date" on the weekends, with the exception of Cornell, which started as a coed school in the middle of the nineteenth century, and the University of Pennsylvania, which had slowly let women seep into various departments. Yale, Dartmouth, and Princeton were 100 percent male in my undergraduate days, Brown and Columbia had coordinate women's colleges, and Radcliffe was still a separate school from Harvard, though women did attend classes with Harvard men. That didn't mean that they were considered in any way equal. (I remember going to some event at the Harvard Club in New York when I was pregnant with Lee and causing a scene because I insisted on going in the main door rather than using the "Ladies Entrance." I wanted to see if they would actually throw a pregnant woman out on the street. They wisely did not, but they weren't happy about letting me in.) Now, not only is the enrollment in these training grounds for "tomorrow's leaders" (think Michelle and Barack Obama, George W. Bush, Bill and Hillary Clinton,

George H. W. Bush, and so on) fairly equally divided between men and women, but—miracle of miracles—four of their presidents are female. The presidency of an Ivy League university is becoming women's work.

The most recent appointment of Drew Gilpin Faust as president of Harvard made national news because it was Harvard and because it came after the Larry Summers controversy, but the spotlight shone on psychologist Judith Rodin's every move in 1994 when she became the first woman to cut through the all-male Ivy as president of the University of Pennsylvania. A big university in a big city with newspapers and television stations waiting to pounce on any misstep presents a challenge to any president, but Rodin was up to it. In her ten years in Philadelphia she did all the things a good college president should do—increasing the endowment, enhancing the faculty, enriching the physical surroundings—but she also reached out to the often hostile Philadelphia community surrounding the urban campus, setting up programs that were helpful to people outside of the university. Rodin worked with other employers in the area, first to clean up the neighborhood and then to plant hundreds of trees. She got involved with the Philadelphia schools and teachers' union, opening a new school in the university neighborhood and providing help from the graduate department of education to other nearby public schools. She helped develop businesses in the area, especially female- and minority-owned businesses, and she used an attractive mortgage program to lure hundreds of faculty and staff members to buy homes in the neighborhood while making sure the locals weren't run out by rising prices through the creation of a fund to support moderately priced rentals. In her first several years as president, Rodin also had a son at home, so life was either work or family. What did that mean for this first ever female Ivy League president? "It's hard to hang out with the girls," she lamented to the college newspaper. "I miss it because I valued the closeness of a lot of my female friendships."

After ten years, Rodin moved on to take over the Rockefeller Foundation, leaving the university in the hands of another woman—political scientist Amy Gutmann. But before Gutmann took over at Penn, a couple of other women had joined Rodin as Ivy League presidents—Shirley Tilghman, a molecular biologist, at the once aggressively male Princeton, and Ruth Simmons, a specialist in French literature, at Brown. Simmons's story is a truly American saga. The twelfth and youngest child of dirt-poor sharecroppers in Grapeland, Texas, she was also the great-granddaughter of slaves. When her family moved to Houston, where her father took a factory job and her mother took in ironing, both made sure their daughter Ruth learned an important lesson: "They helped me to understand something very important: that poverty is not a state of mind nor a definition of one's character, but merely the condition of one's purse," she said in her acceptance speech as the president of Brown

University. At segregated public schools in Houston, her teachers pushed her forward, steering her toward college. But even with all of their pushing, she was a creature of her time, careful to take a backseat to the boys as she graduated from high school in 1963. "I expected that in my relationships with men, I should pretend not to be smart. I never wanted to be valedictorian because I thought it was very important for a boy to be valedictorian."

No pretense could hide her smarts, however, and her teachers helped her clinch an academic scholarship to Dillard University, a one-hundred-and-fifty-year-old school in New Orleans. "The striving of that small black institution and others like it saved this nation from its intolerable tolerance of segregation and racial discrimination, giving rise to a generation of empowered African-American leaders," she said in a 2008 speech in Washington. But it was her junior year at Wellesley, with its female president, that "empowered" her as a woman: "That was defining for me, the notion that women didn't have to play restricted roles, that you didn't have to hold back at all." And she didn't. She went on to Harvard where she earned first a master's degree and then a Ph.D. in Romance languages.

Ruth Simmons quickly went into college administration, moving up the ladder from one college to the next until she was hired by Princeton where, with a couple-of-years detour to serve as provost of Spelman College, a highly regarded black women's school in Atlanta, she eventually was promoted to vice provost. After the president of Princeton asked Simmons to study the state of race relations at the university, her report and its recommendations drew national attention. Soon she was hired as the president of Smith College, the first African American to head a Seven Sisters school. When Brown snatched her away from Smith to become the first African-American president of an Ivy League school, Ruth Simmons said simply, "My ancestors are smiling."

In her acceptance speech, this first woman, first black president told Brown: "I would not have thought it possible for a person of my background to become president of Brown University." But in truth she had worked toward just such a goal all through her academic life, years when she was raising children and practicing patience, something she would advise others to do as well: "Don't rush it, because if you rush it, you'll miss some steps that you'll need later in life. Take your time. Pay attention to your spiritual life, pay attention to your development." That's this remarkable woman's first piece of advice. Her second? "Keep in mind that a job is a job is a job. But, a life is something that is just too short. Live a life that you can be happy with." There it is—the bottom line from generations of women enterprisers.

CONSUMER ADVOCATE

■　　　■　　　■

"ESTHER PETERSON, A DOGGED CONSUMER ADVOCATE WHOSE work has an impact on Americans every time they buy a can of soup or a box of laundry detergent, died today at her home in Washington. She was 91." That was the lead of the obituary in the *New York Times* at the end of 1997. The story behind those words is one of the great tales of an American woman in the twentieth century.

Through much of the time I was growing up in Washington, Esther Peterson was a fixture on the political scene, pitching in for various Democratic administrations, participating in activities at the Women's National Democratic Club, where my mother presided in some years and spent a good deal of time and energy in others. When I returned to town as a reporter in 1977, I found Mrs. Peterson working the corridors of Congress as President Carter's consumer advocate. Her trademark braid wrapped around her head, she marched through the Capitol with a wide grin at the ready, always taking time to greet me even in the middle of an earnest appeal to a recalcitrant lawmaker. I kept looking for an excuse to sit down with her for a lengthy interview. She kept asking me the subject matter, and when I said, "Esther Peterson," she put me off until she had more time.

Finally, in 1993, I got my chance. She was eighty-seven years old and back in government with the latest Democratic administration, this time as a representative to the United Nations. *This Week with David Brinkley* had decided to scrap the usual format for the Christmas program and all of us regulars interviewed someone we found interesting. I chose Esther Peterson. She started her story with her grandmothers, both converted to Mormonism in Denmark. Both made the daring and dangerous passage across the ocean and across the country to Utah. One was part of the Mormon pilgrimage that trekked over the plains. The fact that she took such inspiration from what she called "the inheritance of strength" struck a special chord with me. Whenever I hear modern women complain that they "can't do it all," I think of those women who went on foot across this continent, bearing and burying babies, spinning thread for clothes, creating meals out of nothing, then settling in a place where they had to chop, plow, plant, and build to have a home and a livelihood. They never insisted they couldn't be superwomen. Their experiences provided the context for Esther Peterson's childhood world.

Then there was her mother. One of the first women to attend what was then Brigham Young Academy, her mother was forced to go to work running an old folks' home when her father, the superintendent of schools, became ill. Those many years later her still-proud daughter told me, "She held the family together, economically. There's no doubt about it. But she was a woman." The women who came before her, explained Esther Peterson, inspired her to do what she did—to dedicate her life to educating women so that they could improve their lives and those of their families.

As with many women, hers was anything but a straight path. First, she had to make her own daring journey—to New York City to graduate school at Columbia's Teachers College, unheard of for a good Mormon girl and strongly opposed by her mother because her father had just died and her duty was to be by her mother's side. Esther Peterson's solution? She took her mother with her to New York, where the older woman lasted for about a week and then went home. "But I think I did the right thing"—she was still questioning her decision sixty years later. "It was a matter of encompassing, rather than closing doors, which is something I felt strongly about for a long time in my life."

One of the doors that opened was held by Oliver Peterson, whom she describes as a pipe-smoking socialist—two strikes against him in Mormon Utah. But they married and moved to Boston where she, like other well-brought-up young women, taught at a posh girls' school and, like most women, especially Mormon women, also did volunteer work. It was through that most traditional of paths that Esther Peterson became a labor activist and then a consumer advocate.

She volunteered at the YWCA where she taught working women in the evening. One night when she walked into a nearly empty classroom, Mrs. Peterson learned that her students were on strike, walking the picket line. Their boss had changed the pockets on the housedresses they made, from easy-to-sew squares to heart shapes, much more difficult and time-consuming for the seamstresses. Since they were paid by the dress, this resulted in less pay for more work. More than five decades later, Esther Peterson remembered her reaction: "I thought a strike was simply terrible. I was raised you had bombs in your pockets and you were communists. But Oliver said, 'Go find out. Go find out.' He was wonderful. And I went and saw industrial homework for the first time. I saw what it meant when the whole family sat around one electric lightbulb. I shan't forget it. And I asked about the strike, and I heard about it. So the next morning, I went out, and I was on the picket line and helped them."

That was the beginning. The working women won what came to be called the Heartbreaker Strike with the help of others organized by Esther Peterson into the Citizens' Committee of Concerned Women. They put on their best outfits and stood in the picket line intimidating the Boston police. "Then I became a real labor activist," Mrs. Peterson recalled. "I decided they had to have a voice, the working people. I felt the women were left out, they got the low end of everything, you see. And that was important to me."

So, it was women she organized. First, it was teachers in Massachusetts. Then it was garment workers in New York where she moved for her husband's job. It was World War II, and white women were moving into better factory jobs as black women moved from domestic work into the lower-level jobs the white women left behind. As Esther Peterson went around signing them up for the union, she often brought her toddler daughter with her, showing them that she had the same problems with child care they did. When Oliver Peterson's job moved them to Washington, D.C., his wife became a lobbyist for the Amalgamated Clothing Workers. A female lobbyist for a union in the 1940s! This was the Washington of smoke-filled saloons and snuff-filled spittoons. According to Mrs. Peterson, the CIO chief took one look at her and said, "'What the hell do we do with Esther?' In those days they assigned each person to a congressman or a senator. They said, 'Give her to Kennedy, he won't amount to anything.' And I tell you, my dear, that was the best break I ever had." The labor lobbyist and the future president became fast friends, a liaison that would serve Esther Peterson well in later years.

All this time, while organizing the workforce, Mrs. Peterson was also producing a family. Briefly after the birth of her first child she stayed at home but found herself depressed, and her husband urged her to get back to work. When she wrote her memoirs in the last years of her life, she dedicated the book "to those who are often forgotten, but who have allowed me to enjoy my life as well as my work—my housekeepers, my babysitters, and of course, my family." While pregnant with her fourth child, she was lobbying for an increase in the minimum wage. Senator Claude Pepper told her, "Esther, if it's a boy we'll call it Maxie for maximum hours, if it's a girl we'll call it Minnie for minimum wage." "So you were not only a female lobbyist for a labor union, you were a pregnant female?" I asked incredulously. "You know the thing is that women can do things," came the answer. "Women can do things if they want to, and the men didn't mind my bulge."

Despite her success in the labor movement, Mrs. Peterson was always ready to pick up and go when her husband's job summoned them. That's the kind of thing I think young women often get tied up in knots about, and where her example's useful. Given the life span of most women, we can expect to be in the workforce for decades, if that's what we choose. It makes a lot of sense to me to take advantage of new situations when they present themselves, even if it means taking some time out from a career for a while. It made sense to Esther Peterson as well. So when the State Department asked Oliver Peterson to go to Sweden as a labor attaché in 1948, she didn't hesitate. "Wherever we've gone,

I've found good, interesting things to do. And I knew that would happen here too. And it was a new opportunity. I thought it was simply splendid. Why not?"

In Sweden she learned that domestic workers were covered by labor laws establishing hours, work conditions, and pay. She contacted the Women's Bureau at the U.S. Department of Labor, which asked her to do a study of the Swedish system. Though she was disappointed in how the government handled her report, she marveled at the Swedish system, particularly the job of "mother substitute"—someone to take on the mother's role when she is not able. In her memoir, *Restless,* Peterson says of this job, "It was a great way for middle-aged women who didn't work full-time to make a little extra money and to feel useful. It was a way of assigning value to women's traditional skills. It was an inspiring use of the talents and resources of older women. It was so refreshing to see the recognition of the social and economic value of 'women's work.'" More than sixty years have passed and still nothing similar exists here.

While the family was living in Sweden, Mrs. Peterson's old union buddies asked her to go to London for the International Confederation of Free Trade Unions in 1949, where she was the only female in the U.S. delegation. "Did you find that lonely?" I asked her. "No, I'd always liked men and got along with them. And I think they liked me. You know, I'd give them credit." What a familiar story. My mother always said that you could get anything done as long as you didn't have to get the credit. Not an easy maxim for a politician, but useful.

When the Petersons returned to the United States in 1957, after Esther had established the first international summer school for working women, she returned to the Amalgamated Clothing Workers, where the union tried to pay her two thousand dollars less than the man who had just left the job. The explanation? "Your husband has a job." Needless to say, this woman who had worked her whole adult life for fairness for working women wouldn't accept injustice when it came to her own situation. She fought the union and won. But quickly her interests turned to the presidential campaign of her old friend Jack Kennedy, where she put her formidable organizing skills to work.

With victory came the spoils, somewhat to her embarrassment. As she recounted the conversation with President Kennedy: "He said, 'What do you want?' And I thought, 'My land, what do I want?' My husband was quite ill and I wouldn't leave Washington. So I said, 'Well, the Women's Bureau because I'm interested in women's affairs.' And that's how that developed." What's more, she convinced the president to establish a Commission on the Status of Women, an idea that had been kicked around Congress for a decade. And she persuaded President Kennedy to ask Eleanor Roosevelt to chair the commission, despite Mrs. Roosevelt's support for Adlai Stevenson for the presidential nomination.

As the commission went around the country gathering

information, Peterson used the pulpit of the Women's Bureau to preach to young women about the need to support themselves and to get a decent education. She caught a lot of flak for her efforts, and critics accused her of luring women away from home and hearth, but she learned a lot as well. "I remember going through factories. And I'll never forget one of them, Bendix. Here was this rather puny little man, and a woman was next to him, and she was lifting the thing down onto the conveyor belt. And I said, 'Isn't that his job?' 'He's too small, he can't do it.' And she was paid less than he was."

The commission pushed for a bill in Congress requiring equal pay for women, and when the legislation passed, it was a great moment for Esther Peterson. "One of the last bills that President Kennedy signed was the equal pay bill, 1963. I'm selfish. I call it my bill." She had reason to take that credit. The Kennedy administration thought the measure would be doomed to failure at best, politically unpopular at worst. "I worked awfully hard and the secretary [of labor] said, 'Oh, Esther, equal pay, come on.' I said, 'Well, can I try?' and they said, 'If you do, we'll have nothing to do with it.' Nothing could have been better, because I wanted to lobby it myself and we got it through." The commission also managed to end job designation by sex in the civil service and attacked the issue of property rights for married women. Keep in mind what the laws were in 1963. Some states gave husbands complete control of their wives' earnings, some prohibited direct inheritance by married women, some forbade women to go into business for themselves without the permission of the court. (It was not until 1980 that the U.S. Census Bureau broadened the "head of household" definition to include women. The most recent estimate counts almost 14 million households officially run by women with no husbands on the premises.) Just laying these inequities out for all the world to see made a difference.

It also made a difference that Esther Peterson became assistant secretary of labor for labor standards, making her the highest-ranking woman in government in 1963. (That doesn't say a lot for John F. Kennedy; Dwight Eisenhower had a female in his cabinet.) Even so, she found herself excluded from some meetings she was entitled to attend, and in the spirit of the times, simply took it. She found herself being forced to take a lot over the next few years, after President Johnson created the Consumer Affairs Bureau and named her as the first director. As soon as the president announced her job, the letters from irate customers started pouring in at the rate of about a hundred and fifty a day. But she found that there was no real commitment to the cause in the White House, that she had no staff and no budget. So what did she do? Called on women to volunteer to help her—the League of Women Voters, the Consumers League, and the American Association of University Women—to sort through the mail by subject matter. And then she took on the tough topics of food labels and packaging.

"Oh, and my, the way they went after me," she said with

a laugh thirty years later. "Some of the food manufacturers were saying, 'You're taking the romance out of marketing,' and I remember I said, 'I know lots of better places for romances than the aisles of a supermarket.'" But she saw her battles for what eventually became truth in packaging, truth in advertising, and truth in lending legislation as a continuation of her lifelong interest in educating women to improve their lives. None of it was popular with the business community, or with many members of the Johnson administration, and in the end she was forced out of the executive office building and back into the arms of her labor union. There she tried to bring her consumer-friendly ideas to the union cooperative stores, but there too she met hidebound opposition. Much to her surprise, this woman who had spent her life taking on business interests found a home in private industry.

The owners of the Giant Food chain had heard Esther Peterson's speeches about ingredients and labeling and freshness, her complaints on behalf of consumers that came out of her own role as the family's shopper. As she told the story, the supermarket management came to her with the message "Put up or shut up" and offered her a job as consumer representative. She made a deal that she would do things her way, and if the stores ran into trouble as a result, she would quit. Giant thrived on the goodwill created by Esther Peterson's institution of a consumer bill of rights, freshness dating, unit pricing, ingredient labeling—all long before these things were required by law. Mrs. Peterson asked the questions any shopper wanted answered, like what does it mean when the fish department labels its wares "fresh" and "fancy"? "What's a fancy fish?" asked the new consumer representative. "Well, it's one that's been previously frozen," came back the answer. "So I said, 'Why don't you say so?' 'Oh, no one will buy it.' So I said, 'Then we have a consumer bill of rights except for the fish department.'" That exchange had the effect of correcting the labels, and still the store sold fish. Just give women the information, Mrs. Peterson insisted, and they can make intelligent decisions.

She learned a few home truths about the absurdity of some government regulations as she put in years at Giant, and took her newfound knowledge back to the government when the Democrats returned to power and President Carter asked her, at the age of seventy-one, to serve again as consumer advocate. Her chief mission: passage of legislation creating a government department of consumer affairs. The seasoned lobbyist was horrified at the inexperience and arrogance of the new administration, and not surprised when the legislation failed. But she was able to work with the heads of regulatory agencies to establish energy efficiency labels and fuel economy ratings, a practical response to the energy shortage of the era. She also accomplished some consumer protections for airplane passengers and in the funeral home industry, where she unfortunately shared the customers' experience when her beloved Oliver died in 1979. Throughout all those years, from the time of the Kennedy administration, while she was working for the American consumer she was also caring for her husband, tending him through his long illness.

As he left office, President Carter presented Esther Peterson with the highest-ranking civilian honor—the Medal of Freedom. It seemed a fitting end to a long life of service. But neither the return of Republican rule nor her advancing age stopped her activism. She pushed for an international list of banned products as a representative of the International Consumers Union at the United Nations. Once again she was the butt of much criticism from the business community as she tried to let developing nations know that some of the products coming from America were considered unsafe in this country. I asked how her family handled the attacks. "I think sometimes, 'Oh, Mama, do you have to yell so much?' And especially during the time when I was in the newspaper a lot, 'Oh, Mama, come on.' But they were kind, they knew me for what I am. They said, 'You can't change Mama. She's like she is.'" Thank goodness. What a model. Here was a woman who essentially took the traditional role of teacher and trainer and shopper and used it to make the lives of thousands of women and their families better. And she kept it up until the very end.

When the Democrats came back in with Bill Clinton, she was appointed as a representative to the United Nations, where she told me she saw positive movement in the international organization, which had fallen on rocky times.

"I'm encouraged," she declared in the face of all odds. "But," I protested, "you have spent your life being encouraged." To which this lovely old warrior replied, "Why give up, my dear? One never does, one never should. Wouldn't it be dismal?"

MOTHER/DAUGHTER

■   ■   ■

AT A FAMILY PARTY CELEBRATING MY MOTHER'S APPOINT-
ment as ambassador to the Vatican, my brother stood to
toast her: "Mother, campaign manager, mother, consum-
mate hostess, mother, civil rights advocate, mother, congresswoman, grandmother, convention chairman, mother,
author, great-grandmother, ambassador, mother." Sending
her off to her new challenge in a new country, Tommy had
it right. The dominant note, no matter what others dance
onto the score, no matter what age she and her children
might have reached, remains "mother."

My sister once said, "Motherhood is a function of distance, not time." She meant the immediate worries of mothering, not the fundamentals of the job itself. Barbara's

observation came one night when we had just flown to New Orleans for our Aunt Sissy's funeral. We had arranged to arrive at approximately the same time and then planned to rent a car for the drive to the Gulf Coast of Mississippi, where my aunt had lived. As Barbara started down the escalator to the rent-a-car desk, she heard herself paged. It was my mother, already ensconced at my aunt's, suggesting we ride a shuttle bus instead of driving; she was worried about us traveling at night. Now we were both in our forties at the time. We had each trekked all over the world and managed to survive without helpful hints from our mother. But my sister and I were both also mothers of children who had left home. We knew exactly what our mother was doing, because we did it ourselves. The children would be gone for months, doing who knows what, and we wouldn't worry a bit. The minute they were within proximity we started fretting. Motherhood is forever.

With any luck, mothers adapt, come to understand that their children are no longer children, and treat them accordingly, although we all know cases where that's not true. And in many families eventually the roles reverse, the daughter becomes the one in charge of the mother if she lives long enough, and to some degree that has happened with my mother and me, though no one can be "in charge" of my mother, as political leaders learned over the years. Daughters and daughters-in-law remain the chief caretakers of the elderly in America. Still, even as our lives change, even as our children grow up and go away, that basic mothering instinct, that thing at the core of our very being that impels us to shield them against the world, remains at the ready, even as they become parents themselves. I remember when my son, Lee, was first brought to me after he was born. I can still feel that tiny creature in my young arms, how helpless he was. Almost as physically as I felt the surge of breast milk coming in, I felt a surge of protectiveness seeping through me. My sister recognized that primitive response when my mother resigned from Congress hoping to be able to devote herself full-time to Barbara's care when she was dying.

That was typical. Mamma could always be counted on to come through. Intellectually, I know that she was actually away a lot of the time when we were growing up. She was off campaigning for Daddy or accompanying him on some official trip. She always worked—for him, for the party, for the community. Even so, as I resurrect those childhood pictures in my memory, they all include Mamma. To me, she was the most beautiful woman on earth, and she seemed a constant presence. When I was little I used to fake being sick so I could stay home and play with her. She knew what I was doing, but never let on. Now I realize how many cancellations and rearrangements must have followed in the wake of my announcements that I didn't feel quite up to going to school that day. Some of the time, she'd check in on me and go about her work, leaving me with Emma Cyprian, the housekeeper, who was a much sterner taskmaster. On the rare occasions when I really was sick, Mamma would do something special, like make doll clothes with me, or whip up a bowl of my favorite dessert, floating island, a custard with islands of meringue floating on top. I'm a much more diligent cook than my mother ever was, but to this day I won't make something as time-consuming as floating island.

Barbara, who had appointed herself my teacher, became completely exasperated with me when I was about six years old because she couldn't get across the concept of how to tell time. I remember Mamma making a clock out of a paper plate, with construction-paper hands. We sat at the edge of her bed, going over it again and again. I never caught on. Finally, she just burst out laughing, and it was all okay. I'm sure I remember the episode so well because I was convinced I was a dumbbell, a view my sister was always ready to espouse, until Mamma's laugh just made it all seem silly. That's what she's always done, instill confidence, usually by some action—a hug, a call, a laugh—rather than words. (I'm still not great at telling time, a hazard for a broadcast journalist, so I was grateful when digital clocks came on the scene.) When I was older and various activities kept me at school long after buses and car pools had departed, it was always my mother, the working woman, unlike most of my schoolmates' moms, who would uncomplainingly fetch me and my friends and take us all home or back to our house for the night, thereby silently endorsing our endeavors. It was at our home that people and parties were welcome.

When I was in college, my sister organized a major conference aimed at establishing a domestic Peace Corps. My mother offered to house students who needed rooms. A guy I had met the summer before reserved a space chez Boggs. He and I had dated a few times and I had liked him, but then he didn't call again, so I was curious to see what would happen when we renewed our acquaintance. He had a terrible cough, and in the middle of the night my mother wafted into his room in her negligee and served him a hot toddy. His name was Steve Roberts and he was hooked. He always teases me that he fell in love with my mother first.

Mamma always seemed able to do six things at once, so we and everyone else asked her to do everything. She had such incredible patience. She made all the curtains in the house, most of them complicated silk draperies with linings. If you woke up in the middle of the night, you might find her at the sewing machine, whipping something up after a day at work. For the den, she chose a chintz hunting scene, and carefully cut and sewed it so that the hands, horses' heads, dogs' tails, and whips connected exactly from one panel to the next when the curtains were closed. Not only would I never have the skill to do that, I would have killed myself or someone else as I became completely exasperated in the effort. When we saw the demands she placed on herself, there was no need for her to tell us that we were expected to live up to certain standards as well. And we never wanted to disappoint her. We wore uniforms to school, but to save money she made many of the rest of my sister's and my clothes, including our evening dresses when we were in high school. Sometimes she'd still be stitching us into our dresses, not having had time to install a zipper, while our dates were downstairs getting grilled by Daddy. Years later, when we were no longer embarrassed, we teased her that she had devised a wicked way to ensure our purity.

The most vivid scene of my mother's multidexterity impressed itself forever on me the summer I was getting married. Barbara's husband was in South America, so she came home for a few weeks with her two babies. David, who was about six months old, would not allow you to put him down. He moved from hip to hip, causing my grandmother to dub him "King David." Daddy's big vegetable garden (now tended by Steven) was in full abundance, demanding attention. And Mamma was doing all the cooking for the fifteen hundred guests invited to the wedding. I'm not making this up. Maybe I should repeat that. Mamma was doing all the cooking for fifteen hundred people. I walked into the kitchen after work one day and noticed the signs on the ovens: "Take me out at seven." "Take me out at eight." There at the stove stood my mother, a baby on her hip, a spoon in her hand, and the phone crooked into her neck. In one large, swaying motion she soothed the baby, stirred the pot full of pickles, and dictated a speech into the telephone.

As one of a series of "first woman to . . . ," as in the first woman to be elected to Congress from Louisiana, in 1976 she was chosen as the first woman to preside over a national political convention. There she was, up on the podium, Madison Square Garden jammed with people, TV cameras shooting from every angle, and she heard down below her, "Hey, Maw-Maw." It was an escaped grandchild, whom she quickly scooped up and brought to the podium with her until his wayward parent showed up to claim him. Her priorities never wavered.

A hard act to follow? No kidding. But Mamma never made me feel that way. Instead, she's been a continual source of support and encouragement. When most of my friends felt their mothers slathered on the guilt, my mother was busy erasing mine. One night when my kids were probably still in elementary school, or maybe in junior high, a congressional vote forced me to stay at work late to report it. I found my mother and moaned, "Here it is nine o'clock and I'm still here, I'm worried about my kids." Mamma looked at me intently and insisted, "Cokie, those kids are fine. In fact they're great. Relax." Of course she was right. Think what a relief it was for me essentially to get permission for what I was doing from my mother. Think how unusual it was that I could simply go downstairs in the Capitol to consult her. I missed her terribly when she retired, and missed her even more when at the age of eighty-one she took a new job far from home as the U.S. ambassador to the Vatican, so it's wonderful that she is now close by.

So much of the mother-daughter tension has to do with

an inability to consult, or an unwillingness of either mothers or daughters to admit the value of what the other has to say, I'm convinced of that. Library stacks bulge with books by experts on this subject, I know, but I've done my share of listening over the decades. When mothers who never worked outside the home hear how much their daughters value careers, they take it as a rejection. They are hurt, and often they are jealous as well, feeling they could have "amounted to something" if they had not devoted themselves to their children. But the daughters don't even seem to give them credit for what they did do—raise a family. Rather than ask their mothers, they choose instead to rely on Penelope Leach or Richard Ferber. Instead of days at Grandma's for the kids, it's days at Gymboree or soccer or ballet or jujitsu. So, mothers uncomfortable with this landscape, and feeling left out of it, criticize their daughters and make them mad. And daughters, unsure of themselves and threatened by the criticism, dismiss their mothers and make them sad.

That's not the way it's supposed to work. Mothers and daughters traditionally enjoyed the closest of ties. In the nineteenth century, writes women's historian Carroll Smith-Rosenberg, "expressions of hostility today considered routine on the part of both mothers and daughters seem to have been uncommon indeed." In what was essentially an apprenticeship system, mothers trained their daughters in domesticity. In earlier times, girls worked alongside their mothers in the fields and in the farmhouse. Mom-and-pop shopkeepers often kept the kids behind the counter or waiting tables with them. Girls expected to grow up to be like their mothers and depended on their mothers' and other female relatives' assistance in the process.

Maybe we're on our way back around to that. My daughter and daughter-in-law and their friends genuinely like their mothers, I'm happy to say. Now that they are mothers themselves, I think they have some appreciation for us as well. And we grandmothers like these daughters/mothers enormously. I am so admiring of my daughter and daughter-in-law as moms (their husbands do a good job as dads as well, but this book isn't about men). Rebecca will look at me and laugh when one of her children does something just like she did; but when I get some satisfaction over one of Lee's children acting up in exactly the same way he did, Liza correctly points out that *she* doesn't deserve such behavior. Watching these young women as they engage in the juggling act that we all did, I am awed by their sense of balance. As they keep all the balls in the air, they have an advantage we didn't have—a somewhat more family-friendly workplace. Nowhere near friendly enough, but a lot friendlier than it was when my cohorts and I broke into those buildings. We're not any different from guys, we kept proclaiming, so hire us and promote us. We couldn't then say, Well, actually we are different and we need maternity leave and benefit packages with child care. That took the next crowd coming in after us.

Daughters of women my age have something else going

for them: They have grandmothers. Many of the women a few years younger than I am waited so long to have children, their parents were already elderly by the time the next generation of babies arrived. In contrast, my mother's first grandchild came when she was forty-four, my mother-in-law's, at forty-nine. My daughter loved spending time with these still energetic grandmothers, listening to their different life experiences, extracting the common threads of womanhood. Over sheets of cookie dough or stacks of campaign data, Becca absorbed the wisdom of older women and observed that intelligence does not depend on job descriptions. And now that those grandchildren are parents, their children are incredibly blessed in having their great-grandmothers alive to listen and laugh. My niece Elizabeth's daughters, old enough to get around on their own, sometimes stop by my mother's after school, probably learning a good deal more than they did in the classroom.

My grandmothers were so important to me, I felt so lucky to have them. I'm delighted my daughter feels the same way about hers, and it seems my grandchildren feel the same way about theirs. Coco, my mother's mother, sported spike-heeled shoes and bright red hair. Grandee stuck to sensible brogans and soft white waves. Their lives seemed entirely removed from each other's, but they weren't really. They enjoyed each other's company, in that way that women pulled together over the years often do. The same's true of my mother and mother-in-law. Even in the years when they didn't see each other that often, there was always something between them when they did. At Lee's wedding, when Steve's father had just died my mother literally locked arms with my mother-in-law, so the two of them became a team. Now that they are both living near us, we have many a meal together—often just the two moms and Steve and me at Sunday brunch (I won't pretend that this isn't a logistical challenge; we're talking about 183 years of mother here), or they preside over the whole extended family, four generations strong, at dinners and celebrations. There's a lot of talk these days about the sandwich generation, but in our family it's a club sandwich, with two middle generations helping each other take care of those on either end. I'm very grateful for that and also very well aware it won't be long before I am in the generation on the outer edge, dependent on the women in the middle.

A Mother's Day poll taken not too long ago reveals that American women are closer to their mothers than some of the modern literature would imply. Nearly all talk to their mothers at least once a week (the poll doesn't tell us whether those conversations are pleasant or not), nearly half speak almost every day, and a great many solicit their mothers' advice on child rearing. I find that with both my mother and daughter the conversation can run the gamut from politics to potty training, from radio to recipes. Rebecca seems to have taken ingredients from each of the women in the family as she stirs up her now famous jambalaya.

She loves the political world of my mother and spent the 2008 election covering politics nonstop as a radio journalist. She loves the intellectual and brain-teasing world of Steve's mother, so she joins book clubs and pores over crossword puzzles. She loves my world of journalism and excels at it. She loves the domestic world of all of us and creates wonderful concoctions in the kitchen. And did I mention she's a great mom? Rebecca's one of the most competent, smartest, funniest people I've ever met.

Even when she was a little girl she was willing to exert herself. I remember when she was five she came home from school complaining about the "boring" spelling words—*at, cat, bat.* She had learned them on *Sesame Street* when she was two. I asked if she wanted me to talk to her teacher about it. "No, I'll do it," my five-year-old responded. Her teacher said she could choose her own words from her reading. That night I asked what she had chosen. *"Psychiatrist,"* she answered. Now you know that teacher still thinks I put her up to that.

In the years Becca was in San Francisco, I missed her terribly but I also understood why it was important for her to be at a distance. I think it's easier to establish a marriage away from the expectations of extended family and to take the first steps in motherhood without someone peering over your shoulder. Though my head believed she was doing exactly the right thing, my heart couldn't be convinced to accept her distance, or her brother's when Lee moved to London. Even though it was an incredibly busy time of my life and even though the "kids" had been gone from home for almost a decade when they moved so far away, those years of thousands of miles and several time zones between me and my children were tough ones because, no matter what else I'd ever done, from the time they were born my first definition of self had been "mother." From the moment I watched the first baby emerge from my body, to the moment I watched the second walk down the aisle to form a new family, my first responsibility was to those two people.

When they're little people, you can actually feel that responsibility in your weary bones; there's no such thing as calling in sick on mommyhood. How do they survive? Lee was a pretty cautious kid, but Becca was death-defying. At thirteen months, she managed to put a rent-a-car into gear and drove out of a drive-in laundry in California. I went tearing out to save her by driving the car into another one. You can imagine the accident report: age of driver, one year. That was just the beginning with her. But as every mother knows, the fear of physical danger is nothing compared with the worry about emotional upset. When they were in school, a bell rang in my head every day at three o'clock—the kids were home, what was happening? I'd call and get the usual responses. Conversation with son: "How are you?" "Fine." "What did you do today?" "Not much." Conversation with daughter: "How are you?" "Great." (Or terrible, or some superlative.) "What did you do today?" "Well, in first period we did. . . ." Half an hour later I was still holding the phone at my ear. Lee would occasionally bare his soul, but only when I was away. He'd see my phone number, call me at one or two in the morning, and pour out his problems. Then he'd go happily to sleep, leaving me wide awake in some motel room in Iowa, my arms aching I wanted so much to hold him. He told me later that he would never have talked to me so frankly had I been home sleeping in my own bed.

With a daughter it was different. I'm not saying that Becca told me her innermost thoughts, but we did talk a lot. We were also buddies—in the kitchen, in the shopping malls, on the phone. When she left for college I felt like I had said good-bye to one of my best friends. I don't know what I would have done if I didn't have a busy work life to occupy me. The kids were awfully generous about coming home, and bringing their friends around. Lee moved back in for a few months after college when he was between apartments and I found out that all of this talk about boomerang kids misses an essential point. They are able to come home because we like them, and they like us. The famous generation gap's now nothing more than a crack.

Even after Lee moved out he still came home for Sunday-night dinners. After a while he started bringing Liza McDonald with him. He had first met her years before when they were teenage pages at the Capitol. Now she was back here as a reporter, of all things. Briefly, Liza worked with me at ABC, where she became my friend, too. As I got to know her well, I knew this was a young woman any mother would die for, and I was scared to death Lee might blow it. Fortunately, Lee proved again that he's no dummy, and Liza is a dear daughter to me. And Becca's guy, Dan Hartman, is a great one, so we're lucky indeed.

As a mother, watching your children go off to start their own families is both heartening and hard. Now it's someone else who occupies first place in their lives, someone else they will call to say they've arrived safely. And they have suddenly become part of a whole new family tree; we are but one of their extended branches. Maybe consciously, maybe not, both our kids married people whose parents have now been married for more than forty years. These are families in which people love each other and love our children. And of course we are all jointly gaga over our grandchildren. We are also grateful that our daughters are mothers, because there's no other role as demanding, as terrifying, as maddening, and as rewarding as that of mother.

I always wanted children, but not until they were actually part of my life did I realize that I could love that fiercely, or get that angry. Even when the kids were very little, I always found them fascinating people. Every parent says this because it's true—it's remarkable how formed those personalities are from the minute they pop. Mothers and mothers-in-law can tell you some home truths about yourself and your spouse as you embark on bringing up those boisterous babies. Grandmothers and great-grandmothers can tell you some truths about your mother as well.

E NTREPRENEUR

▨   ▨   ▨

WHEN I WAS AT WELLESLEY, I USED TO STUDY AT THE HAR-
vard Business School library. It was right across the river
from Steve's dorm, so at the end of a day at the books, I
could wander over and hope to "run into" him. I don't
know why they let Wellesley women into the library in
those years. They didn't allow women into the business
school itself until 1963. That's right. Even so, somehow as a
sex we managed; women have thrived in business, particularly as business owners, calling somewhat into question
that hallowed Harvard degree.

The most recent numbers from the Center for Women's
Business Research tell us that women own 40 percent of all
U.S. businesses, a total of about 8 million enterprises. They

employ about 13 million people and bring in revenues of almost $2 trillion. The fastest-growing firms in America are owned by women of color, and once a woman starts a business, she's more likely to keep it going than is her male counterpart.

We know that women have been in business at least since the "good wife" of Proverbs who "considers a field and buys it" and "perceives that her merchandise is profitable." In this country women were licensed as tavern owners in Massachusetts as early as the 1600s, and women regularly ran businesses while their husbands were away at sea, or at war, or when they were widowed. In a wonderful book called *Daughters of America; or, Women of the Century,* written in 1883, the author, Phebe Hanaford, quotes from a contemporary New York newspaper: "Some curious facts relative to various businesses carried on in New York City by women are made known in the latest directory published at the metropolis. The proportion of men to women in business where the women stand as their own representatives is 4,479 women to 37,203 men." More than 10 percent! The paper goes on to cite the businesses—billiard and lager-beer saloon owners, blacksmith, druggist, pawnbroker, wood-engraver, doctor.

Most of these early American entrepreneurs have been lost in the mists of history. But a few survived the anonymity of women in the annals, and some of their tales are worth telling or retelling. One is Margaret Brent, called "Gentleman Margaret Brent" because the men of seventeenth-century Maryland didn't know how else to address her. When she arrived in the colony in 1638, she was already acting as a lawyer. (How that happened the histories don't tell us.) Then, thanks to the intervention of her cousin, Lord Baltimore, she and her sister took possession of a sizable tract of land, and thanks to the indebtedness of her brother, she acquired his very substantial property as well. (Had she been married, she would not have been able to own anything, a common-law rule that did not change until the late nineteenth century in most parts of the country.) Margaret Brent continued to amass land, and therefore power, and soon became legal counsel to the governor. Can you imagine the judges and opposing lawyers? What were they supposed to do with this woman? They had no choice but to pay attention to her, which turned out to be a good thing for Maryland. The civil war in England meant a summons to Governor Calvert to return to the motherland. While he was there, two Virginians, one of them, by the way, my direct ancestor William Claiborne, took control of Maryland. They were Protestants; Maryland was Catholic. Calvert came back, raised an army to retake the colony, and then died, first naming Margaret Brent as executor of his estate. The soldiers Calvert had hired had not been paid, or even fed, and an uprising was on the horizon. Miss Brent first held them at bay by importing corn from Virginia and slaughtering some of her own cattle to feed them. Then, when the Calvert estate turned out not to be sufficient to compensate the soldiers, she used her power of attorney for the new governor to draw on the estate of the colony's proprietor, Lord Baltimore. She sold enough cattle to pay the mutinous army, and the soldiers went away peacefully. When from his perch in England Lord Baltimore strenuously objected to the Maryland Assembly, he was disappointed in the response. Instead of rebuking Brent, the assemblymen commended her, saying, "It was better for the Colony's safety at that time in her hands than in any man's else in the whole Province." The assembly was ready to praise her, but not to give her a vote, which she demanded as a freeholder. In fact, she asked for two votes, one for herself and one for her client, Governor Green. It was one of the few fights she lost. Before retiring to Virginia at the age of fifty-six, she was involved in 124 court cases, including many jury trials, and she won them all.

Women inventors pop up often in the history books. The flirty and feisty Catherine Littlefield Greene, wife of Revolutionary War hero Nathanael Greene, never received any credit for the cotton gin, which was patented in 1794. But a Web site of the Massachusetts Institute of Technology's School of Engineering concluded: "Experts on invention agree that Eli Whitney could not have developed the cotton gin—the quintessential American invention—without Greene's advice. In fact, some believe that Whitney stole the credit for what was essentially Greene's invention." In 1809 Mary Kies became the first woman actually to win a patent for her method of weaving straw with silk. With the country bristling under an embargo on imported goods, First Lady Dolley Madison praised and promoted Kies's domestically made hats. By 1840, approximately twenty women held patents for ingenious inventions, mostly having to do with improving their lives as cooks, cleaners, and seamstresses.

One woman who followed in the footsteps of these early inventors was Lillian Moller Gilbreth, called "the mother of modern management." She started cooking and cleaning for twelve children in the early twentieth century (one of her children wrote *Cheaper by the Dozen*) and, in addition to her writing and lecturing, worked with her husband on time management. Some ways to save time? The electric food mixer and the trash can with step-on lid-opener—she was awarded patents for both. After her husband died, Gilbreth joined the faculty of Purdue University in 1935 as a professor of management and the first female professor in the engineering school (though her graduate degrees were in literature and psychology). As the first woman member of the American Society of Mechanical Engineers, she worked for General Electric, where she interviewed more than four thousand women as part of an effort to design the perfect kitchen, paying particular attention to the needs of the disabled.

It was out of her experience as a secretary that Bette Nesmith Graham created a product that turned into a multimillion-dollar business. A frustrated artist and a single mother supporting a son (Michael Nesmith of the Monkees fame!), Bette worked at a Texas bank typing letters and documents. Irritated that she had to start over again every time she made a mistake, she looked for some way to make corrections. As an artist, she realized that you painted over your accidents, so she tried to come up with a similar solution to typing errors. She did—in her kitchen blender (which, by the way, was invented by a man). When the other secretaries started asking for some of her magic potion, she put the dyed-to-match-the-stationery water-based tempera in a bottle labeled Mistake Out. In 1956 she started a company selling the bottles out of her kitchen, with the help of the future musician and his young friends. Renaming it Liquid Paper, she obtained a trademark as well as a patent, and by 1967 it was a million-dollar business. The next year she moved out of the kitchen into a production plant where, with still-fresh memories of life as a single mother, she set up a child care center and library for her employees and sold a million little bottles of the doctored paint. International sales followed as Bette Graham (who remarried in 1962 and again divorced in 1975) moved into a yet larger facility and hired yet more people. In 1979, not long before word processors would make Liquid Paper far less necessary, she sold the company for $47.5 million. She gave much of her money to the foundations she established to help women and girls by offering programs like career counseling for unwed mothers, shelter and support for battered women, and college scholarships for older women. Bette Nesmith Graham died the next year. She was fifty-six.

Madam C. J. Walker used her very different experience from either Bette Nesmith's or Lillian Gilbreth's to create her highly successful enterprise. I first learned about this fellow Louisianian from my ABC News friend and colleague A'Lelia Bundles, Ms. Walker's great-great-granddaughter, who has written a wonderful book about her exceptional ancestor. In 1867 Sarah Breedlove was the first member of her family born to freedom. But release from slavery did not mean release from the no-exit life of poverty of a Louisiana sharecropper. Orphaned at age seven, married at fourteen, soon a mother, and widowed at twenty, she supported herself and her daughter, A'Lelia, with backbreaking work as a washerwoman for almost twenty years, first in Vicksburg, then in Saint Louis. She managed miraculously to send her daughter to school, and joined the missionary society at church, where she met for the first time black people with education, culture, and money. The Saint Louis World's Fair in 1904 introduced the young woman not only to prominent black leaders but also to beautiful black women. Women with hair. Like many poor people with bad diets, Sarah Breedlove McWilliams had lost much of her hair, in an era when the Gibson Girl, with her upswept mane, was the standard of beauty. McWilliams's determination to grow her hair turned her into the first American black woman millionaire.

She claimed that the formula for her hair products came to her in a dream. It might have come to her by trial and error in the pharmacy where she worked after moving to Denver to be with her brother's widow and children. Wherever the formula came from, it worked. Her own luxurious head of hair attested to that fact better than any advertisement. After marrying journalist C. J. Walker, she christened the product Madam C. J. Walker's Wonderful Hair Grower and sold it door-to-door. Thanks to Walker's help in publicizing it and her own talent for self-promotion, the Walker System, as she called it, became a huge success. Madam Walker then started her own cosmetics company, hiring thousands of women to sell her products, and became famous the world over. She eventually moved the headquarters to Indianapolis, but she first set up house in Harlem. Her daughter, A'Lelia, later ran part of the mansion, known as the Dark Tower, as a salon for black artists and intellectuals.

The flamboyant Madam Walker not only made vast sums of money, she also gave it away. Born a sharecropper's daughter, she died a renowned philanthropist. It's hard to wrap your mind around this kind of achievement. The hurdles she had to vault—poverty, ignorance, racism, sexism—made her a great believer in self-help. But Walker believed in helping others as well, contributing to the NAACP plus dozens of black charities and providing girls with scholarships to the Tuskegee Institute. She promoted female talent and spurred on the sales of the some three thousand women who worked for her with prizes and bonuses. The charter of her business specified that only a woman could serve as president. And when she died at age fifty-one, her daughter took over the cosmetics empire.

Hiring and promoting women also characterized Margaret Rudkin's approach to a successful business. I love this story because it's rooted in such practicality. A doctor in 1937 told Mrs. Rudkin that he thought her son's asthma might stem from an allergy to chemical additives in commercially baked bread. So, like a good mother, she started baking her own. But first she did a little homework, as all good girls do, studying nutrition and holistic medicine. She came up with a whole wheat bread made with all fresh ingredients, and her son seemed to get better. At least he improved enough that the doctor ordered the bread for himself and other patients. Thus was born a little enterprise called Pepperidge Farm.

First Rudkin sold her breads to doctors through the mail. Soon she had to hire a neighbor to help her bake, and expanded the kitchen into the garage and stable. It wasn't long before she was peddling her products wholesale. And peddle she did. She'd walk into a store with bread, butter, and a knife, give a taste to the owner, and hook him. Two years after she started the business, Pepperidge Farm was selling twenty-five thousand loaves of bread a week. Expansion was impossible during World War II, but once the war was over, a new plant started turning out four thousand loaves of bread an hour. Yet Rudkin still insisted the dough be hand kneaded and the ingredients fresh. She hired women because she simply thought they were better at baking bread than men. Hard work was expected, and above-average pay provided. Like Madam Walker, Maggie Rudkin promoted herself to a fare-thee-well and she had the advantage of a new invention called television. But it was a *Reader's Digest* article that put her on the international map. Despite constant growth in the business, she insisted the quality stay high and the bread fresh. A two-day shelf life was the maximum she allowed, but then Rudkin did something ingenious with the stale leftovers—she made stuffing, and sold it at a profit. Next it was cookies, created from a Belgian recipe after she and her husband went around Europe with the tough task of tasting cookies wherever they went. When I was a new bride I always served Pepperidge Farm Pirouettes with my desserts; I thought they were quite elegant and sophisticated looking. By the time Maggie Rudkin sold the bakery she had started as a response to her little boy's asthma, it was a company with $32 million in annual sales. Campbell Soup bought it in 1960 for $28 million in Campbell's stock. Though she was clearly an astute businesswoman, Rudkin understood the tenor of the times. She marketed herself as the ultimate housewife and her multimillion-dollar business as a homey little bakery where no one had to feel threatened by a woman in charge.

But the time has come when anyone who feels threatened

by a woman in charge will simply have to get over it. It's happening too slowly for me—only fourteen of the Fortune 500 companies have female chief executive officers—but women are taking the helm or helping steer at more and more businesses. I have been amazed at how women holding high positions in the business world can now fill a conference hall. And they make a difference in the bottom line. A 2008 study by the McKinsey management consultant company confirmed what others had shown: More women in top management means more money in the bank. And, as in politics, these women often bring different perspectives to the job. Anne Sweeney, head of the Disney–ABC Television Group, is regularly rated as one of the most powerful women in the world by *Forbes* and *Fortune,* but I think of her as the boss who sends out e-mails on the first day of school and Halloween urging her employees to take time with their children on those days—if their supervisors agree, of course. Meg Whitman, who grew the online auction site eBay into a multi*billion*-dollar business, once explained her style of leadership: "It's different from traditional leadership," she said. "It's usually: What does the center want to do? It's command and control. At eBay, it's a collaborative network."

Collaboration is what Anne Mulcahy talks about as well. Plucked from her stints in sales and human resources, she was a surprise pick to take over failing and flailing Xerox in 2001 when the company was on the verge of going under. With incredible determination and grit she fought off the advisers who told her to throw in the towel and declare bankruptcy. Concerned about the families that worked for Xerox, she took the long view, investing in research and development against the advice of all the more experienced financial hands, and she turned the company completely around. "I became really good at asking for help, I had to," she said when she was honored as the first woman to be chosen Chief Executive of the Year. "In the end the culture saved us. Because we're not hierarchical." I don't think it's an accident that all of these extremely successful, collaborative women are mothers. So is Indra Nooyi, who as the head of Pepsi is ranked the third most powerful woman in the world by *Forbes*. Having made business decisions that have brought in billions of dollars in profits, Nooyi is now trying to turn the soft drink giant into a health food giant—a plan she is sure will be good for the company as well as the country. She never loses sight of the people she is selling to—they could be her children in America, or her mother in India, who gets a call from her CEO daughter daily. This sari-wearing corporate titan has a message for the rest of us: "Don't forget that you're a person, don't forget you're a mother, don't forget you're a wife, don't forget you're a daughter." Mothers not only know that they have to take the long view (how else could they get through child-raising?) but they also tell their children that they can't have everything they want the minute they want it. Not a bad message for employees, stockholders, and boards of directors as well.

Breaking into those boards of directors remains a stubborn barrier to women in business as we settle into the twenty-first century. Even as white men decline in their percentage of the population, they are still the overwhelming majority on boards. Only 15 percent of the people sitting in those power-dispensing rooms are female, only 3 percent are women of color. And some of the same females sit on several boards, so the actual numbers of women are even smaller than the percentages would imply. A recent study on how women change corporate boards reveals that they show up more often than their male counterparts, eventually shaming the men into attending more often as well, and they hold the CEOs more accountable for performance. Not at all surprising—there's that mother thing again. Corporate boards are the place where the ultimate power resides when it comes to the work life of many Americans. With women making up almost half of the labor force, it's past time for us to have more say in the world of work—to create a culture that reflects the fact that we are mothers, wives, and daughters. Then we might, just might, be able to stop this endless argument about a woman's place.

A Woman's Place

　　▨　　　▨　　　▨

"A WOMAN'S PLACE IS IN THE HOUSE . . . AND IN THE SEN-
ate," the T-shirts and buttons proclaim at women's political
events. "A Woman's Place Is in Uniform," trumpets a book
about women in the military. "A woman's place is at the
typewriter," declared *Fortune* magazine back in 1935. That
was convenient for the economy and so it was decreed. A
few years later a woman's place was in the factory or in the
nursing corps because that was essential for the war effort.
Then a woman's place was in the home. And now? A woman's place is anywhere she wants it to be. Fine, but who's
taking care of the children? That's the question that keeps us
roiled up over this issue, as we learned yet again in the 2008
political campaign. When Alaska governor Sarah Palin, the

mother of five children, was nominated for vice president, headlines around the country screamed, "Palin Candidacy Sparks Wave of 'Mommy Wars,'" "Live from the RNC: Mommy Wars 2.0," "Palin Story Fuels 'Mommy Wars.'" News organizations couldn't get enough of the story, which elicited dozens of responses on their Web sites—almost all from women—who kept battling in their comments. These arguments drive me crazy. Women proclaiming that Palin had no business running for high office because she had kids at home never raise an eyebrow about fathers of young children hitting the campaign trail for a few years.

When my colleague Charlie Gibson asked Sarah Palin: "Is it sexist for people to ask how can somebody manage a family of seven and the vice presidency?" my answer was a resounding "Yes! Unless you ask it of male candidates as well." Her response was more politic: "That question is kind of irrelevant because it's accepted of course you can be the vice president and you can raise a family." As long as you're a man. Charlie told the Alaska governor that when he posed the question on the ABC Web site, fifteen *thousand* people weighed in. Clearly the country still has its collective knickers in a knot over mothers' work. I thought that the entry of so many women into politics would put an end to the double standard, but clearly that's not the case. Back when Pat Schroeder was first running for Congress in the early 1970s and kept being asked "What about the children?" she gave an answer that remains my personal favorite: "Jim and I get up very early—about 6:00 A.M. We bathe and dress the children and feed them a wonderful breakfast. Then we put them in the freezer, leave for work, and when we come home, we defrost them. And we all have a lovely dinner together. They're great!"

Despite attempts like Schroeder's to ridicule this whole debate, it just won't go away. I can't get over how quick people—usually women—are to pass judgment, condemning any woman they deem to have "abandoned" her children. Look at a comment posted on a *Saturday Evening Post* story after swimmer Dara Torres qualified for the Beijing Olympics: "The time that Torres spends each day in training is time apart from her daughter. Is that a good thing?" Many Americans still think the answer to that question is no. In 2007 when Pew Research asked: "Is the trend toward more mothers of young children working outside the home a good thing or a bad thing for our society?", 41 percent said bad, only 22 percent good, with about a third saying it made no difference. This at a time when almost two-thirds of the mothers of preschool children are in the workforce! So all of those women are doing a "bad thing"?

Wait a minute. Hasn't "our society" required welfare mothers to go to work, insisting that it's better for the children to have an employed parent? Could we make up our minds here, please? No, probably not, because here we are in the twenty-first century still confused about a woman's place. We're confused because we know that no matter what else a woman is doing, she's also caretaking, and we worry that a woman "out at work" might leave someone, especially her children, without care. That's what's at the heart of this sometimes vicious, sometimes absurd argument. Sure, a lot of other much less noble attitudes also underlie these debates. Plenty of people still think that women are just plain uppity and they see a woman's place as someplace to put her. But I think it's the question of the children, and now old people as well, that truly troubles us. And women with children often find whatever choice they make uncomfortable.

That wasn't always true. For most of human history men and women worked together in the same place, and each one's work complemented the other's. No one thought the farmer's job was more important than the farm wife's. Neither could manage without the other. Teenage relatives often moved in to help care for the children, to protect them from household hazards like open fires while the busy mother made the soap and the candles, spun the yarn, pieced together the clothes, fixed the food. Women gathered together to help with large chores, and visited as they worked. They also congregated to attend to births and deaths, taking comfort from one another's company. Whenever I think of the courage it took to leave everything and everyone behind to come to this continent in the early years of colonization, I am struck by the fortitude of those settlers. First the trip across the ocean, then in later generations the trek across the continent, required women to "do it all." The history of the movement west is one of extraordinary men and women overcoming incredible odds together.

It was the industrial revolution that changed everything. Men went out to work for wages, and they were paid for the hours they put in, not the tasks they completed. (Poor women went into the factories, or to domestic work, as well. In 1850 women comprised 13 percent of the paid labor force; this question of women's work, as Dorothy Height reminded us, is one directly related to economic class.) Suddenly, what women did at home lost its value because there was no paycheck attached. Repetitive housework replaced home manufacture as women's crafts moved into assembly-line production. And that's what we've been struggling with ever since. Doing work that is economically rewarded and socially recognized means leaving home. That's changing with the information revolution, as machines make it possible to work just about anywhere. But I think it's unlikely to alter the fact that women aren't paid for their jobs as nurturers, and it still leaves women at home isolated from other women.

It's important, I think, for young women today to understand that they are not the first generation to deal with these questions. That's part of the reason I've tried in this little book to give some sense of the scope of women's work over many generations, to give today's women a glimpse of women who have gone before them. But knowing that you're not the first to have to cope with a problem doesn't necessarily make solving it any easier. And for reasons that

I don't fully understand, women make one another's lives harder by trying to impose their own choices on their sisters. Again, it's important to be clear-eyed here that we are talking only about women privileged enough to have choices. Most women work for the same reason most men do—because they have to, they have no other option. If society makes some statement about mothers and children, it should relate to all mothers and children.

Over the last forty years, I've watched this argument go full circle. When I was in high school and college, my friends' mothers did not work, and there was definitely a stigma attached to female employment. My own mother escaped it because she worked for and with my father, which was acceptable. Keep in mind, this was not long after World War II, when there was an organized effort to get women out of the workplace. A women's magazine article in 1951 (the year I was in third grade) lists the pros and cons of the author's decision to quit her office job. Among the items she counts as "lost," along with "the sense of personal achievement" and "praise for a good piece of work," is "baseless vanity. I realize now (and still blush over it) that during my working days I felt that my ability to earn was an additional flower in my wreath of accomplishments." On the "found" list, along with "normalcy" and "intimacy," is "Improved Appearance. Shinier hair, nicer hands, better manicures, are the products of those chance twenty-minute periods that turn up in the busiest days of women who don't go to business." That would have convinced me.

With the advent of modern feminism, it was women at home who were looked down upon by their fellow females. What were they doing with their educations? How could they allow themselves to be so dependent on a male? Didn't they know he could up and leave them penniless at any moment? The women's movement gave lip service to the concept of choice, but didn't mean it. The strong message: Women, to have any worth, you must go to work, get a paycheck, and show that you are just like a man.

Now there's been a swing back to stigmatizing the at-work woman if she is a mother, and the media highlights anecdotes of accomplished women who have decided to detour off the fast lane, declaring an "Opt Out Revolution." Women in these stories, and remember, we're talking here only about wealthy women who can afford it, wax eloquent about the satisfaction of staying home with the kids. Some take direct aim at their sisters still on the job. It can all get awfully tedious, and veer toward the ridiculous. I remember reading an article in our local newspaper whose author opined that a working mother wouldn't be able to bake with the children and hand down the cookie recipes from generation to generation. I thought of my cabinet full of cookie cutters— Christmas cookie cutters, Hanukkah cookie cutters, valentine cookie cutters, Halloween cookie cutters, dinosaur cookie cutters—and the hours I have put in rolling the dough, overseeing the decoration, first with my children, now with my grandchildren ("No, you can't dump a whole bottle of sprinkles on one cookie"), and all I could do was laugh. Then I got angry. Who was she to question my choices? And why did she want to? To validate her own.

Obviously, there's good reason to be concerned about children, and if this country's ready to have a serious conversation about children, I'm all for it. But that conversation goes to far more fundamental questions than how some middle- and upper-middle-class women spend a few years of their lives. If we truly want to concern ourselves with America's kids, let's talk about children who go to bed hungry every night in this richest nation on earth. Let's talk about children who are denied a decent education because of rotten public schools. Let's talk about children who are shoved from foster home to foster home. Let's talk about children who are in danger from their parents and their neighborhoods. Let's talk about children whose parents use them as pawns in domestic wars. Let's talk about children who are incarcerated. Let's talk about children who are lonely. Let's talk about children who have no hope for their futures. Children with two parents married to each other who care enough about them to worry about work versus home are already well ahead of the game. I don't mean to belittle the difficulty in making those choices; I'm just trying to put them in perspective.

Women would do well to take the long view in making personal decisions, as we always have. The number of years we have children at home, particularly preschool children, is few. The number of years available to move ahead in the workforce is many, assuming we live full life spans. Putting career on the back, or at least the middle, burner in the years children are small makes a lot of sense to me. That doesn't necessarily mean staying home full-time. For me, that would have been a disaster. I need to work for my spiritual and emotional well-being, and while that might not be admirable, it's true. In interim periods between jobs I've suffered genuine depression, and believe me, that's not good for the children. I was a better mother because I worked.

But there were times along the way when I turned down good jobs because they weren't appropriate for my family. As we were leaving Los Angeles, some feelers came my way about anchoring a new TV newscast. I didn't even pursue them, because we were moving to Greece. While I was in Greece, the CBS foreign editor talked to me about being the network's "woman in Europe." It sounded very glamorous, but I would have been traveling all the time. Steven's job required nonstop travel, so it didn't seem at all fair to the kids for both of us to be gone constantly. I said no.

That's not to say that there have never been times my family's suffered because of my job. Of course there were. And the kids resented the long wait for dinner every night, the calls saying that we'd be home, and then the calls saying we'd be later than expected. I'm sure there were times that it would have been more comfortable and comforting for them if I had been home after school, times that it would have been helpful to them if I were available to drive them on errands or to see friends. As your kids get older they don't want you around most of the time, but when they want you, they want you. Unfortunately, there's no way to schedule those times, they just happen. You can schedule the things you know about, and there Steven and I had a pretty good track record. We were there for everything important—the adjustments to new schools, the activities, the performances, and I was very involved in the PTAs over the years. As we look back on it, there's only one big event Steven and I missed, at least only one that we know about—Becca's first dance.

It was the weekend before the 1984 election. I was in Los Angeles, Steve was in Chicago. We each called home to discover that Becca had gone to the homecoming dance. She was a freshman, her date a senior. Lee was decidedly unforthcoming with the details. He didn't know who was driving, when the invitation was issued, what time she would be home. "What was she wearing?" I asked. "Something blue and shiny of yours," he replied. I felt guilty and angry that I wasn't there, cheated out of my daughter's first dance, worried that no rules had been set with the boy. Of course, there was an adult staying with the kids, but that's not the same as a parent when it comes to your first big date. Steve and I each kept calling to check on her. It got later and later, still no Becca. We called each other in a panic and stayed on the phone so long that we realized she couldn't get through to us if she did show up. (This was before cell phones, remember.) When she finally checked in she explained that she was the last kid in the car to be delivered home because her parents were away and it wouldn't matter. Oh great. Luckily, she was a good kid, as was her brother.

So yes, there were times that my work got in the way of my family. And there were times when my family got in the way of my work. It will continue to do so. Children might be our first responsibility, but let's not kid ourselves: Women care for the whole family, which includes the family of friends. Polls show that upwards of 90 percent of working women claim primary responsibility for child care. And this nurturing goes on forever. My thirtieth college reunion class book includes this entry: "George's parents are still in good health and maintain active lives. We think it is remarkable that his 81-year-old father and 78-year-old mother look after George's 100-year-old grandmother who still lives alone in her Wisconsin farmhouse."

When my sister was sick, work took a backseat. When Nina Totenberg's husband was sick, I spent time every day with her and him that I would otherwise have spent at work. In one year my father-in-law died, both of my kids got married, and my mother sold her apartment in Washington and moved to Rome, which involved packing up fifty-seven years of her life. Each one of those events took precedence over my work. Becca's wedding came close to being a full-time job, but since both she and I had those already, it couldn't be. Now, with an elderly mother and mother-in-law in town, much of my time is spent with them, and at this stage of my life I am fortunate to be in a much more flexible situation than most working women. That, of course, wasn't always the case. There were years in there when I needed a far more family-friendly workplace and much more help with the caretaking. So do most women. As Nancy Pelosi put it in her book, "For our society to benefit from the full contribution of women at home and at work we must make a national decision to expand access to quality childcare." I would add elder care as well. And it's not just individual people who need our care. The community as a whole deserves the time and talent of its women.

Just a few weeks before she died at the age of ninety-seven, former senator Margaret Chase Smith wrote an introduction to the book *Outstanding Women Members of Congress*. " 'Where is the proper place of women?' is a question I have often been asked," she begins. "The quizzers have asked this question ambitiously, defiantly, hopefully—and just plain inquisitively. But it has been asked so many times in so many ways and by so many types of people that, of necessity, my answer has had to transcend the normal and understandable prejudice that a woman might have. My answer is short and simple—woman's proper place is everywhere. Individually it is where the particular woman is happiest and best fitted—in the home as wives and mothers; in organized civic, business and professional groups; in industry and business, both management and labor; and in government and politics. Generally, if there is any proper place for women today, it is that of alert and responsible citizens in the fullest sense of the word."

Because our communities and our country need us just as the children do, the country requires the services of women soldiers and politicians and businesswomen and clubwomen and sportswomen and scientists and reformers and consumer and civil rights and human rights activists and women helping other women get off welfare and nurses and nuns. The country needs us to be sisters and aunts and friends and mothers and grandmothers and daughters and wives, first in the literal sense and then in the figurative one—sisters to society, caretakers. Women can complain forever about how our devotion to those roles is not remunerated, that society doesn't compensate us for our nurturing. And frankly, I don't think we'll ever solve that problem. If we want public recognition and financial reward we will continue to have to "do it all." But that's not such a terrible thing. One piece of advice for young women: Don't worry about it so much. There are times when life is emotionally and physically exhausting, and times when sleep deprivation seems likely to do you in, but you'll make it. Women are tough. I heard from dozens of them after this book was first published, good-humoredly describing how over the years they managed to keep all of the balls in the air. Here's a classic example from an Ohio woman: "Defining a woman's role today was made easy for me a few years ago as I hung up a sign by my back door, in a spot where I could see it each day as I returned from my job as a high school secretary. It is a simple wooden plaque, showing two women in old-fashioned garb, at two stationary tubs, doing laundry. The words are 'A woman's place is in the home . . . and she should go there directly after work!' That was my motto as I worked for thirty-two years, raised three children with a cooperative husband, took care of my father in our home for twenty-seven years until he died at age eighty-nine, and served as a support system for a mother-in-law who moved to our town after her husband died."

A woman's place is something I've been puzzling about most of my adult life. It surprised me, when I unearthed a journal where I occasionally jotted down my thoughts while we were living in Greece, to find something I had written when I was thirty-three years old and contemplating our family's next move. "No one writes about women like me, and we probably form a large group, who daily make the choice about our career, family, etc. It's not a one-time decision, but a continual one. And we can get so trapped by any alternative—the pure kid, pure work or balance. So can a man, of course, but in nothing like the same way." The balancing act is one we must constantly recalibrate—what works one year doesn't work the next; what works for one child doesn't work for another; when you think you've cleared the decks for a project on the job, something happens in the family; just when you've put aside time to be with your kids or your mother, something happens at work. It's foolish to make too many plans. Life gets in the way. Look, I know I've been lucky. I've been blessed with a happy marriage, four fabulous kids and kids-in-law, six healthy grandchildren, two long-lived mothers, the many joys of family and friendship, and a fine, fulfilling career. By living on this earth long enough, I've learned that clichés are clichés because they are true. It's true that you'll only have one opportunity to witness your baby's first step, to hold your dying sister's hand, to see your mother credentialed by the Pope, to hold your mother-in-law as she learns of her husband's death, to have your son introduce you to your first grandchild, to celebrate more than forty years with your husband. There will always be another job.

So what is a woman's place? For most women it's many places, different places at different times. For almost all women, it's the place of nurturer, whether for the planet or one small creature on it. We learned it from our mothers, both in word and in deed; we teach it to our daughters in the knowledge that they must carry on the culture and care for it. Even as they go forward in this new millennium, knowing things we never knew, they will be connected back to those women in Marathon, Greece. From that continuity they will derive the strength to make their place wherever they think it should be.

Acknowledgments

ANY TIME I UNDERTAKE A PROJECT OF ANY SIZE, IT MEANS my friends and family have undertaken it as well. This one was no exception, so there are many to thank. My dear friend Ann Charnley has been my buddy for more than forty years. When I first wrote this book, I knew she was just the right person to ask for help in researching these themes, and she has since found fabulous women for all of the books that came after this one. Heather Gilbert was also a great help on this revised edition, as were my daughter-in-law, Liza Roberts, and my daughter, Rebecca Roberts, who came up with great ideas about interesting women. At HarperCollins my friend and editor Claire Wachtel pushed me to do this book in the first place, somehow turning me into an author, and we have had a wonderful run ever since. We could not have done this edition without her able assistant, Julia Novitch. At Morrow, publicist DeeDee DeBartlo is not only terrific at her job, but she's good fun, Kim Lewis continues to put up with my up-against-the-deadline delivery of manuscripts, and publisher Lisa Gallagher cheers me on. I am blessed with great "girl bosses" who are my friends and supporters, as well as gifted managers—Robin Sproul at ABC and Ellen McDonnell at NPR. Kim Roellig keeps the rest of my life going so that when I'm involved in a project like this not too much falls through the cracks; she and I have been a team for many years now and for that I am most grateful. Bob Barnett is more than a lawyer, he's a friend, and he never points me in the wrong direction. Of course it would be impossible to do any piece of work like this without a lot of understanding on the home front. My husband, Steven, though writing his own book at the same time, has been his usual supportive and loving self. And to my mother, mother-in-law, daughter, daughter-in-law, sister, sisters-in-law, great-grandmothers, grandmothers, great-aunts, aunts, tantes, teachers, nieces, great-nieces, cousins, and friends, plus American women past and present—thank you for providing the material.

Suggested Reading

Baxandall, Rosalyn, and Linda Gordon. *America's Working Women: A Documentary History from 1600 to the Present.* New York: W. W. Norton, 1995.

Berlage, Gai Ingham. *Women in Baseball: The Forgotten History.* Westport, CT: Praeger, 1994.

Bird, Caroline. *Enterprising Women.* New York: W. W. Norton, 1976.

Cayleff, Susan E. *Babe: The Life and Legend of Babe Didrikson Zaharias.* Urbana: University of Illinois Press, 1996.

Chafe, William H. *The Paradox of Change: American Women in the 20th Century.* New York: Oxford University Press, 1991.

Committee on House Administration of the U.S. House of Representatives. *Women in Congress, 1917–2006.* Washington, DC: U.S. Government Printing Office, 2006, and accompanying Web site http://womenincongress.house.gov.

Cott, Nancy F. *The Bonds of Womanhood: "Woman's Sphere" in New England, 1780–1835.* 2nd ed. New Haven: Yale University Press, 1997.

————, gen. ed. *The Young Oxford History of Women in the United States.* New York: Oxford University Press, 1994.

Cowan, Ruth Schwartz. *More Work for Mother: The Ironies of Household Technology from the Open Hearth to the Microwave.* New York: Basic Books, 1983.

Eisenhart, Margaret A., and Elizabeth Finkel, with Linda Behm, Nancy Lawrence, and Karen Tonso. *Women's Science: Learning and Succeeding from the Margins.* Chicago: University of Chicago Press, 1999.

Evans, Sara M. *Born for Liberty: A History of Women in America.* New York: Free Press, 1997.

Faust, Drew Gilpin. *Mothers of Invention: Women of the Slaveholding South in the American Civil War.* Chapel Hill: University of North Carolina Press, 1996.

Franck, Irene M., and David M. Brownstone. *Women's World: A Timeline of Women in History.* New York: Harper Perennial, 1995.

Guttman, Allen. *Women's Sports: A History.* New York: Columbia University Press, 1991.

Hanaford, Phebe A. *Daughters of America; or, Women of the Century.* Augusta, ME: True, 1883.

Hartmann, Susan M. *The Home Front and Beyond: American Women in the 1940s.* Boston: Twayne Publishing, 1982.

Height, Dorothy. *Open Wide the Freedom Gates: A Memoir.* New York: Public Affairs, 2003.

Heinemann, Sue. *Timelines of American Women's History.* New York: Roundtable Press Books, Perigee Books, 1996.

Hoffman, Ronald, and Peter J. Albert, eds. *Women in the Age of the American Revolution.* Charlottesville: University of Virginia Press, United States Capitol Historical Society, 1989.

Holmstedt, Kirsten. *Band of Sisters: American Women at War in Iraq.* Mechanicsburg, PA: Stackpole Books, 2008.

James, Edward T., ed. *Notable American Women 1607–1950: A Biographical Dictionary.* 3 vols. Cambridge: Harvard University Press, Belknap Press, 1971.

Juster, Norton. *So Sweet to Labor: Rural Women in America 1865–1895.* New York: Viking Press, 1979.

Klein, Ethel. *Gender Politics: From Consciousness to Mass Politics.* Cambridge: Harvard University Press, 1984.

Larson, C. Kay. *'Til I Come Marching Home: A Brief History of American Women in World War II.* Pasadena, MD: Minerva Press, 1995.

Lerner, Gerda. *The Majority Finds Its Past: Placing Women in History.* New York: Oxford University Press, 1979.

Litoff, Judy Barrett, and David C. Smith. *We're in This War, Too: World War II Letters from American Women in Uniform.* New York: Oxford University Press, 1994.

Matthews, Glenna. *Just a Housewife: The Rise and Fall of Domesticity in America.* New York: Oxford University Press, 1987.

Miller, Ernestine. *Making Her Mark: Firsts and Milestones in Women's Sports.* New York: McGraw-Hill, Contemporary Books, 2002.

Nelson, Maria Burton. *Embracing Victory: Life Lessons in Competition and Compassion.* New York: William Morrow, 1998.

Pelosi, Nancy, with Amy Hill Hearth. *Know Your Power: A Message to America's Daughters.* New York: Doubleday, 2008.

Peterson, Esther, and Winifred Conkling. *Restless: The Memoirs of Labor and Consumer Activist Esther Peterson.* Washington, DC: Caring Publishing, 1997.

Riley, Glenda, and Richard W. Etulain. *By Grit and Grace: Eleven Women Who Shaped the American West.* Golden, CO: Fulcrum Publishing, 1997.

Roberts, Cokie. *Founding Mothers: The Women Who Raised Our Nation.* New York: William Morrow, 2004.

———. *Ladies of Liberty: The Women Who Shaped Our Nation.* New York: William Morrow, 2008.

Robertson, Nan. *The Girls in the Balcony.* New York: Fawcett Columbine, 1992.

Schroeder, Pat. *24 Years of House Work . . . and the Place Is Still a Mess.* Kansas City: Andrews McMeel Publishing, 1998.

Sherr, Lynn. *Failure Is Impossible.* New York: Times Books, 1995.

Sherr, Lynn, and Jurate Kazickas. *Susan B. Anthony Slept Here.* New York: Times Books, 1976, 1994.

Smith, Lissa, ed. *Nike Is a Goddess: The History of Women in Sports.* New York: Atlantic Monthly Press, 1998.

Smith-Rosenberg, Carroll. *Disorderly Conduct: Visions of Gender in Victorian America.* New York: Oxford University Press, 1985.

Swanson, Richard A., and Betty Spears. *History of Sport and Physical Education in the United States.* 4th ed. New York: WCB/McGraw-Hill, 1995.

Thomas, Helen. *Front Row at the White House.* New York: Scribner, 1999.

Washington, Shirley. *Outstanding Women Members of Congress.* Washington, D.C.: U.S. Capitol Historical Society, 1995.

Whitney, Catherine, et al. *Nine and Counting: The Women of the Senate.* New York: William Morrow, 2000.

Yount, Lisa. *A to Z of Women in Science and Math.* New York: Facts on File, 1999.

BOOKS BY
COKIE ROBERTS

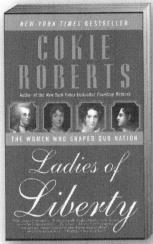

ISBN 978-0-06-078235-1

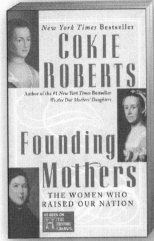

ISBN 978-0-06-009026-5

ISBN 978-0-06-095954-8

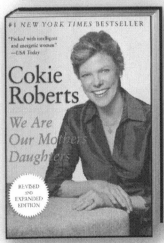

ISBN 978-0-06-174195-1

Made in the USA
Middletown, DE
18 September 2019